365 Days of Slow Cooking for Two:

Easy and Healthy Slow Cooker Cookbook
for Beginners
(From Appetizers to Desserts).

by
Sophia Bexley

Hi!

Thank you for purchasing our book. Your support and trust in us are much appreciated. **Use this QR code** to get an electronic variant of this book as **a GIFT from us**! No more will cookbooks be ruined with unsightly splodges or splashes of cooking sauces, with our e-version.

How to use the book?

In each recipe you can see a QR code. After scanning this code, you will see a photo of the finished dish.

Why do we use QR codes in our books?

1) It is modern, innovative, and eco-friendly.

2) It saves book production costs, reduces energy, paint, and paper costs. This is our contribution to the care of the planet and the environment.

3) All this allows us to make the price of the book lower for buyers. Plus, you get not only the paperback, but also the electronic version of the book absolutely for free!

4) Thank you for contributing to the care of the environment with us!

Contents

Introduction

Slow cooking never gets old and it is as relevant today as it was hundreds of years ago. Today we don't do it on a wood fire using Dutch ovens or a cooking pot, we do it in electric slow cookers. These cookers have made it easier to slow cook all sorts of meals at home without constant supervision, you can go out to run some errands with the slow cooker on and it will safely cook the meal without giving you constant worries of your food being burnt or overcooked. The automatic temperature and cooking time control system make the slow cooker a must-have for all households. If you happen to have a slow cooker or are thinking about getting one then this cookbook contains great ideas to cook a variety of meals using nothing but a slow cooker.

Why Slow Cooker meals?

Hands-off cooking, energy conservation, and bringing out the taste in most dishes are just a few of the advantages of using a slow cooker. They also encourage healthy cooking and are more user-friendly than other kitchen gadgets. Slow cookers are a lifesaver for many busy families nowadays since they can prepare dinner while everyone is at work or school, and when it's time for supper, the hot meal will be waiting for them at home. Let's see in how many other ways slow cookers help you:

Perfect Meals With Hands-Off Cooking

Slow cookers, unlike other appliances, enable you to add in your recipe ingredients and let them cook on their own, which is a terrific feature since it allows you to focus on other things while your meal cooks. All you have to do is place the food in the slow cooker, select your favorite settings, and leave the rest to the slow cooker. This function is very handy for individuals who have hectic schedules and don't have a lot of time to spend cooking dinner. Once the cooking time is over, the machine automatically switches to KEEP WARM mode and that prevents the unattended food from burning and overcooking.

Bring Out the Flavors

Slow cooking is well-known for bringing out the best taste in a meal. It mixes the varied qualities of the ingredients, resulting in a burst of aromas and real, additive-free flavours. Because the components simmer at such low temperatures, a slow cooker allows for appropriate flavour distribution, resulting in a mouth-watering dish.

Tenderized Meat

With a slow cooker at your side, you can quickly tenderize tough meats or inexpensive meat cuts, leaving them soft, tender, juicy and flavorful after a long cooking duration, which is why slow cookers are considered great for cooking beef, venison or lamb stews and curries. You can tenderize less-lean beef, roast, or chuck steaks in a slow cooker without paying more for the more costly cuts.

Easy To Use and Learn

It is easy to cook a slow-cooker meal. To operate your slow cooker, you don't need much experience with the cooking appliance. All you have to do now is add everything into the slow cooker, choose your favorite settings, and put it on. A slow cooker may produce a flavorsome delight even if you've never used one before since it doesn't take long to learn how to operate it. It is sufficient to read the user handbook or follow the recipe in this cookbook to prepare a delicacy. For first-timers, a slow cooker cookbook is very helpful.

Healthy Cooking

High heat is known for breaking down nutrients in meals, lowering the overall nutritional value of a cuisine. High temperatures might cause the release of potentially toxic chemical compounds, which can cause kidney problems and even diabetes. Slow cooking allows nutrients to be retained while preventing the release of unwanted, potentially poisonous compounds due to the extremely low temperatures used. Because you won't be cooking at high temperatures using slow cooking, the meals cooked will be much healthier compared to fried or baked meals.

Fresh Hot Food For Serving

It takes longer for food cooked in a slow cooker to cool down quickly. Most new slow cookers include 'stay warm' settings that keep your meal warm after it has finished cooking. So, at the time of serving, you dish out a sizzling hot meal straight from the cooker.

The Ultimate Time Saver

In a slow cooker, you can cook the fanciest of the meals with minimum supervision. When you're occupied with other activities, a slow cooker is a terrific way to cook food. It doesn't need much attention, so it's ideal for when you're too tired to accomplish anything else or simply want to avoid adding another duty to your to-do list. When all of the ingredients are placed in this gadget and turned on, there's no need to keep an eye on it or check it every few minutes - in fact; many recipes recommend not removing the lid at all during the cooking process!

Breakfast Recipes

Banana French Toasts

Cook time: 5 hours | Serves: 4 | Per Serving: Calories 385, Carbs 38g, Fat 23.4g, Protein 13.2g

Ingredients:

- Eggs – 3
- Milk – ½ C.
- Powdered stevia – ½ tbsp.
- Ground cinnamon – ½ tsp.
- Vanilla extract – ½ tbsp.
- Bananas – 2, peeled and sliced
- Fresh lemon juice – ½ tbsp.
- Whole-wheat baguette slices – 8 (1-inch thick)
- Butter – 2 tbsp. melted
- Pecans – ½ C. chopped

Directions:

1) Grease the pot of a slow cooker.
2) In a large-sized bowl, add eggs, milk, stevia, cinnamon and vanilla and beat well until blended.
3) In another bowl, place banana slices and drizzle with lemon juice evenly.
4) Arrange baguette slices in the pot of prepared slow cooker.
5) Pour egg mixture over slices evenly.
6) Arrange banana slices over each baguette slice.
7) Pour melted butter over banana slices and top with pecans evenly.
8) Close the lid of slow cooker and set on "Low" setting for 4-5 hours.
9) After cooking time is finished, uncover the slow cooker and serve warm.

Pumpkin Porridge

Cook time: 5 hours | Serves: 4 | Per Serving: Calories 96, Carbs 11.1g, Fat 5.5g, Protein 3.3g

Ingredients:

- Unsweetened almond milk – ½ C. divided
- Pumpkin – 1 lb. peeled and cubed into ½-inch size
- Liquid stevia – 3-4 drops
- Ground allspice – ¼ tsp.
- Ground cinnamon – ½ tbsp.
- Ground nutmeg – ½ tsp.
- Walnuts – ¼ C. chopped

Directions:

1) In the pot of a slow cooker, place ½ C. of almond milk and remaining ingredients and stir to blend.
2) Close the lid of slow cooker and set on "Low" setting for 4-5 hours.
3) After cooking time is finished, uncover the slow cooker and stir in the remaining almond milk.
4) With a potato masher, mash the mixture completely.
5) Serve warm with the topping of walnuts.

Apple & Squash Porridge

Cook time: 8 hours | Serves: 4 | Per Serving: Calories 178, Carbs 25.6g, Fat 7.9g, Protein 5.5g

Ingredients:

- Raw almonds – ¼ C. soaked for 12 hours and drained
- Raw walnuts – ¼ C. soaked for 12 hours and drained
- Apple – 1, peeled, cored and cubed
- Medium butternut squash – ½, peeled and cubed
- Applesauce – 1 tbsp.
- Ground cinnamon – 1 tsp.
- Ground ginger – ¼ tsp.
- Ground nutmeg – ¼ tsp.
- Fat-free milk – ½ C.

Directions:

1) In a small-sized food processor, add nuts and pulse until a meal like texture forms.
2) In the pot of a slow cooker, add nut meal and remaining ingredients and gently stir to combine.
3) Close the lid of slow cooker and set on "Low" setting for 8 hours.
4) After cooking time is finished, uncover the slow cooker and with a potato masher, mash the mixture slightly.
5) Serve warm.

Coconut & Pecan Porridge

Cook time: 6 hours | Serves: 4 | Per Serving: Calories 317, Carbs 7.5g, Fat 31.5g, Protein 5.8g

Ingredients:

- Pecan halves – 1 C.
- Unsweetened dried coconut shreds – ½ C.
- Pumpkin seeds – ¼ C. shelled
- Water – 1 C.
- Unsalted butter – 2 tsp. melted
- Liquid stevia – 4-6 drops

Directions:

1) In a food processor, add pecans, coconut and pumpkin seeds and pulse for about 30 seconds.
2) In the pot of a slow cooker, place the pecan mixture and remaining ingredients and stir to blend.
3) Close the lid of slow cooker and set on "High" setting for 1 hour.
4) After cooking time is finished, uncover the slow cooker and serve warm.

Barley Porridge

Cook time: 8 hours | Serves: 4 | Per Serving: Calories 274, Carbs 48.4g, Fat 7g, Protein 7.4g

Ingredients:

- Pearl barley – 1 C.
- Unsweetened almond milk – 2 C.
- Water – 2 C.
- Maple syrup – 2 tbsp.
- Fresh orange zest – 2 tsp. grated
- Ground cinnamon – 1 tsp.
- Ground ginger – 1 tsp.
- Salt – ¼ tsp.
- Walnuts – ¼ C. chopped

Directions:

1) In the pot of a slow cooker, place all ingredients and stir to blend.
2) Close the lid of slow cooker and set on "Low" setting for 8 hours.
3) After cooking time is finished, uncover the slow cooker and serve warm.

Blueberry Millet Porridge

Cook time: 4 hours | Serves: 4 | Per Serving: Calories 341, Carbs 64.2g, Fat 2.5g, Protein 14.3g

Ingredients:

- Millet – 1 C.
- Fresh blueberries – 3 C.
- Fat-free milk – 4 C.

Directions:

1) In the pot of a slow cooker, place all ingredients and stir to blend.
2) Close the lid of slow cooker and set on "High" setting for 4 hours.
3) After cooking time is finished, uncover the slow cooker and serve warm.

Fruity Quinoa Porridge

Cook time: 8 hours | Serves: 4 | Per Serving: Calories 268, Carbs 40.6g, Fat 9.1g, Protein 8.5g

Ingredients:

- Quinoa – 1 C. rinsed
- Large apple – 1, peeled, cored and chopped
- Unsweetened almond milk – 2 C.
- Unsweetened applesauce – ½ C.
- Ground cinnamon – 1 tsp.
- Walnuts – 4 tbsp. chopped

Directions:

1) Grease the pot of a slow cooker.
2) In the prepared slow cooker, add all ingredients except for walnuts and stir to blend.
3) Close the lid of slow cooker and set on "Low" setting for 8 hours.
4) After cooking time is finished, uncover the slow cooker and serve warm with the topping of walnuts.

Coconut Cereal

Cook time: 8 hours | Serves: 4 | Per Serving: Calories 98, Carbs 5g, Fat 8.5g, Protein 1.4g

Ingredients:

- Unsweetened coconut – 1 C. shredded
- Unsweetened almond milk – 2 C.
- Water – 2 C.
- Coconut flour – 1/3 C. divided
- Ground cinnamon – ½ tsp.
- Vanilla extract – ½ tsp.
- Liquid stevia – ¼ tsp.

Directions:

1) In the pot of a slow cooker, add the coconut, almond milk, water, ¼ C. of coconut flour and cinnamon and with a wire whisk, mix well blended.
2) Close the lid of slow cooker and set on "Low" setting for 8 hours.
3) After cooking time is finished, uncover the slow cooker and stir in the remaining coconut flour, vanilla extract and stevia until blended well.
4) Immediately cover the slow cooker for about 2-3 minutes.
5) Serve warm.

Raisins Oatmeal

Cook time: 6 hours | Serves: 4 | Per Serving: Calories 62, Carbs 12.4g, Fat 0.9g, Protein 1.7g

Ingredients:

- Steel-cut oats – 1 C.
- Water – 3 C.
- Maple syrup – 2-4 tbsp.
- Raisins – 3 tbsp.

Directions:

1) In the pot of a slow cooker, blend together all ingredients except for raisins.
2) Close the lid of slow cooker and set on "Low" setting for 5½-6 hours.
3) After cooking time is finished, uncover the slow cooker and immediately stir in the maple syrup and raisins.
4) Serve warm.

Pumpkin Oatmeal

Cook time: 8 hours | Serves: 4 | Per Serving: Calories 361, Carbs 18.1g, Fat 29.8g, Protein 4.2g

Ingredients:

- Steel-cut oats – 1 C.
- Chia seeds – 1 tbsp.
- Canned pumpkin puree – 1 C.
- Pumpkin pie spice – 1 tsp.
- Unsalted butter – ¼ C.
- Unsweetened coconut milk – 2 C.
- Unsweetened applesauce – ¼ C.
- Vanilla extract – ¼ tsp.

Directions:

1) In the pot of a slow cooker, blend together all ingredients.
2) Close the lid of slow cooker and set on "Low" setting for 6-8 hours.
3) After cooking time is finished, uncover the slow cooker and serve warm.

Chicken & Bell Pepper Omelet

Cook time: 2¾ hours | Serves: 4 | Per Serving: Calories 188, Carbs 6.5g, Fat 9.4g, Protein 19.5g

Ingredients:

- Milk – ½ C.
- Eggs – 6
- Garlic clove – 1, minced
- Dried parsley – ½ tsp. crushed
- Red pepper flakes – ¼ tsp. crushed
- Salt and ground black pepper, as required
- Cooked chicken – ¾ C. chopped
- Bell pepper – 1, seeded and sliced thinly
- Small white onion – 1, finely chopped
- Mozzarella cheese – 1 C. shredded

Directions:

1) Lightly grease the pot of a slow cooker.
2) In a bowl, add the milk, eggs, garlic, parsley, red pepper flakes, salt and black pepper and beat until blended well.
3) In the prepared slow cooker, place the egg mixture.
4) Add the chicken, bell pepper and onion and stir to blend.
5) Close the lid of slow cooker and set on "High" setting for 2½ hours.

6) After cooking time is finished, uncover the slow cooker and sprinkle the omelet with cheese evenly.
7) Again, Close the lid of slow cooker and set on "High" setting for 15 minutes.
8) After cooking time is finished, uncover the slow cooker and transfer the omelet onto a plate.
9) Cut into equal-sized wedges and serve hot.

Artichoke Frittata

Cook time: 2 hours │Serves: 4 │ Per Serving: Calories 229, Carbs 15.3g, Fat 12.9g, Protein 15.8g

Ingredients:

- Eggs – 6
- Ground black pepper, as required
- Roasted red peppers – 1 (10-oz.) jar, drained and chopped
- Artichoke hearts – 1 (12-oz.) can, drained and chopped
- Scallion – 3 tbsp. chopped
- Feta cheese – 4 oz. crumbled

Directions:

1) Grease the pot of a slow cooker.
2) In a bowl, add eggs and black pepper and beat well.
3) Place red peppers, artichoke hearts and scallion into the prepared slow cooker.
4) Pour egg mixture over vegetables and gently stir to combine.
5) Top with cheese evenly.
6) Close the lid of slow cooker and set on "High" setting for 2 hours.
7) After cooking time is finished, uncover the slow cooker and transfer the frittata onto a platter.
8) Cut into equal-sized wedges and serve hot.

Chicken & Veggies Frittata

Cook time: 3 hours │Serves: 4 │ Per Serving: Calories 215, Carbs 5g, Fat 10.3g, Protein 25.3g

Ingredients:

- Eggs – 8
- Dried parsley –½ tsp.
- Pinch of garlic powder
- Salt and ground black pepper, as required
- Cooked chicken – 1 1/3 C. finely chopped
- Bell pepper – 1½ C. seeded and chopped
- Frozen chopped spinach – ¾ C. thawed and squeezed
- Yellow onion – ¼ C. chopped

Directions:

1) Grease the pot of a slow cooker.
2) In a bowl, add the eggs, parsley, garlic powder, salt and black pepper and beat well.
3) Place the remaining ingredients into the prepared slow cooker.
4) Pour the egg mixture over the chicken mixture and gently stir to blend.
5) Close the lid of the slow cooker and set on "High" setting for 3 hours.
6) After cooking time is finished, uncover the slow cooker and transfer the frittata onto a platter.
7) Cut into equal-sized wedges and serve hot.

Spinach Quiche

Cook time: 4 hours | Serves: 4 | Per Serving: Calories 215, Carbs 10.1g, Fat 13.2g, Protein 15.6g

Ingredients:

- Frozen chopped spinach – 10 oz. thawed and squeezed
- Feta cheese – 4 oz. shredded
- Milk – 2 C.
- Eggs – 4
- Red pepper flakes – ¼ tsp. crushed
- Salt and ground black pepper, as required

Directions:

1) In the pot of a slow cooker, add all the ingredients and mix well until blended.
2) Close the lid of slow cooker and set on "Low" setting for 4 hours.
3) After cooking time is finished, uncover the slow cooker and transfer the quiche onto a platter.
4) Cut into equal-sized wedges and serve hot.

Eggs with Tomatoes

Cook time: 8 hours 25 minutes | Serves: 4 | Per Serving: Calories 170, Carbs 11g, Fat 10.6g, Protein 9.2g

Ingredients:

- Olive oil – 1 tbsp.
- Medium onion – 1, chopped
- Garlic cloves – 2, minced
- Jalapeño pepper – 1, seeded and finely chopped
- Smoked paprika – 2 tsp.
- Ground cumin – 1 tsp.
- Salt, as required
- Diced tomatoes – 1 (26-oz.) can
- Eggs – 4
- Feta cheese – ¼ C. crumbled

Directions:

1) In a non-stick frying pan, melt butter over medium heat and sauté onion for about 3-4 minutes.
2) Add the onion, garlic, jalapeño, paprika, cumin and salt and cook for about 1 minute.
3) Transfer the onion mixture into the pot of a slow cooker.
4) Add the tomatoes and stir to combine.
5) Close the lid of slow cooker and set on "Low" setting for 8 hours.
6) After cooking time is finished, uncover the slow cooker and with the back of a spoon, make 4 wells in the tomato mixture.
7) Carefully crack 1 egg in each well.
8) Close the lid of the slow cooker and set on "High" setting for 20 minutes.
9) After cooking time is finished, uncover the slow cooker and serve hot with the topping of cheese.

Lunch Recipes

Beet & Feta Salad

Cook time: 4 hours | Serves: 4 | Per Serving: Calories 189, Carbs 14.2g, Fat 13.4g, Protein 6.6g

Ingredients:

For Salad:

- Medium red beets – 4, trimmed
- Olive oil – 1 tbsp.
- Fresh baby spinach – 6 C.
- Fresh lemon zest – ¼ tsp. grated finely
- Feta cheese – ¼ C. crumbled
- Pumpkin seeds – 4 tbsp.

For Dressing:

- Garlic cloves – 2, minced
- Fresh cilantro – 1 tbsp. minced
- Extra-virgin olive oil – 2 tbsp.
- Fresh lemon juice – 1 tbsp.
- Ground black pepper, as required

Directions:

1) Place 1 beet over a piece of foil paper and drizzle each with oil.
2) Wrap each foil around the beet to seal it.
3) Arrange the foil packets in the pot of a slow cooker.
4) Close the lid of slow cooker and set on "High" setting for 3-4 hours.
5) After cooking time is finished, uncover the slow cooker and transfer the beets into a salad bowl. Let them cool slightly.
6) Peel and cut the beets into desired-sized pieces.
7) Add remaining salad ingredients and mix.
8) In another bowl, add all dressing ingredients and beat until blended well.
9) Pour dressing over beets and gently toss to coat well.
10) Serve immediately.

Stuffed Spaghetti Squash

Cook time: 8¼ hours | Serves: 4 | Per Serving: Calories 143, Carbs 28.2g, Fat 3.2g, Protein 5.1g

Ingredients:

- Diced tomatoes – 1 (14½-oz.) can with juices
- Fresh mushrooms – 1 C. sliced
- Spaghetti squash – 1 (3-lb.), halved lengthwise and seeded
- Dried oregano – ½ tsp.
- Salt and ground black pepper, as required
- Mozzarella cheese – ¾ C. shredded

Directions:

1) Grease the pot of a slow cooker.
2) In a bowl, blend together the tomatoes and mushrooms.
3) Arrange the squash halves onto a smooth surface cut side-up.
4) Fill each squash half with tomato mixture and then sprinkle with oregano, salt and black pepper.
5) Arrange the squash halves into the prepared slow cooker.
6) Close the lid of slow cooker and set on "Low" setting for 6-8 hours.
7) After cooking time is finished, uncover the slow cooker and sprinkle the top of each squash half with cheese.
8) Close the lid of slow cooker and set on "Low" setting for 10-15 minutes.
9) After cooking time is finished, uncover the slow cooker and transfer the squash halves onto a platter.
10) Cut each squash half into 2 portions and serve.

Butternut Squash with Fruit

Cook time: 4 hours | Serves: 4 | Per Serving: Calories 143, Carbs 37.2g, Fat 0.4g, Protein 2.1g

Ingredients:

- Small apples – 2, peeled, cored and chopped
- Butternut squash – 1½ lb. peeled, seeded and cubed
- Dried cranberries – ¼ C.
- Small onion – 1, chopped
- Ground cinnamon – 1 tsp.
- Garlic powder – ¼ tsp.
- Ground black pepper, as required

Directions:

1) In the pot of a slow cooker, blend together all ingredients.
2) Close the lid of slow cooker and set on "High" setting for 4 hours.
3) After cooking time is finished, uncover the slow cooker and serve hot.

Feta Veggie Combo

Cook time: 3 hours | Serves: 4 | Per Serving: Calories 209, Carbs 25.1g, Fat 10.3g, Protein 8.5g

Ingredients:

- Olive oil – 1 tbsp.
- Eggplant – 1 lb. peeled and cut into 1-inch cubes
- Small zucchini – 1, chopped
- Small yellow squash – 1, chopped
- Large bell pepper – 1, seeded and chopped
- Large red onion – 1, chopped
- Tomatoes – 4, chopped
- Garlic cloves – 4, minced
- Dried basil – 2 tsp.
- Salt and ground black pepper, as required
- Feta cheese – 4 oz. crumbled

Directions:

1) In the pot of a slow cooker, place all the ingredients except for cheese and stir to combine.
2) Close the lid of slow cooker and set on "High" setting for 3 hours.
3) After cooking time is finished, uncover the slow cooker and serve hot with the topping of feta cheese.

Tofu with Broccoli

Cook time: 4¼ hours | Serves: 4 | Per Serving: Calories 156, Carbs 15.6g, Fat 6.1g, Protein 13.7g

Ingredients:

- Olive oil – 2 tbsp.
- Extra-firm tofu – 1 lb. pressed, drained and cubed
- Small onion – 1, chopped
- Fresh ginger – 2 tsp. minced
- Garlic cloves – 3, minced
- Tomato sauce – 1 (8-oz.) can
- Hoisin sauce – ¼ C.
- Balsamic vinegar – 2 tbsp.
- Applesauce – 1 tbsp.
- Mustard – 1 tbsp.
- Red pepper flakes – ½ tsp. crushed
- Ground black pepper, as required
- Water – 2 tbsp.
- Small broccoli florets – 4 C.

Directions:

1) In a large wok, heat oil over medium heat and stir fry the tofu for about 2 minutes per side.
2) Transfer the tofu into a bowl.
3) In the same wok, add onion and sauté for about 5-7 minutes.
4) Add ginger and garlic and sauté for 1 minute more.
5) Add in remaining ingredients and cook for about 2-3 minutes, stirring frequently.
6) Grease the pot of the slow cooker.
7) Add tofu and sauce mixture into the prepared slow cooker and stir to combine.
8) Close the lid of slow cooker and set on "High" setting for 3 hours.
9) After cooking time is finished, uncover the slow cooker and stir in broccoli.
10) Again, close the lid of slow cooker and set on "High" setting for 1 hour.
11) After cooking time is finished, uncover the slow cooker and serve hot.

Oats & Sausage Pilaf

Cook time: 9 hours 10 minutes │Serves: 4 │ Per Serving: Calories 323, Carbs 19.6g, Fat 15.9g, Protein 24g

Ingredients:

- Unsalted butter – 1 tbsp.
- Pork sausage – 1 lb.
- Steel-cut oats – 2 C.
- Low-sodium chicken broth – 8½ C.
- Pinch of garlic powder
- Ground black pepper, as required

Directions:

1) In a non-stick wok, melt butter over medium heat and cook sausage for about 10 minutes or until browned.
2) With a slotted spoon, transfer the sausage onto a cutting board and then cut into ½-inch slices.
3) Add cooked sausage and remaining ingredients into the pot of a slow cooker and stir to combine.
4) Close the lid of slow cooker and set on "Low" setting for 8-9 hours.
5) After cooking time is finished, uncover the slow cooker and serve warm.

Beans in Yogurt Sauce

Cook time: 10 hours 5 minutes | Serves: 4 | Per Serving: Calories 322, Carbs 52.3g, Fat 5.5g, Protein 18.2g

Ingredients:

- Canola oil – 1 tbsp.
- Small white onion – 1, chopped
- Fresh ginger – 1 tsp. minced
- Garlic – 1 tsp. minced
- Curry powder – 2 tsp.
- Ground cumin – ½ tsp.
- Red pepper flakes – ¼ tsp. crushed
- Tomato paste – 4 oz.
- Plain Greek yogurt – 6 oz.
- Water – ¼ C.
- Pinto beans – 1½ (15-oz.) cans, rinsed and drained
- Fresh parsley – 2 tbsp. chopped

Directions:

1) In a non-stick wok, heat oil over medium heat and sauté the onion for about 3-4 minutes.
2) Add the ginger, garlic, curry powder and spices and sauté for about 1 minute.
3) Stir in tomato paste, yogurt and water and immediately remove from the heat.
4) In the pot of a slow cooker, place the beans.
5) Pour the yogurt mixture over beans and gently stir to combine.
6) Close the lid of the slow cooker and set on "Low" setting for 8-10 hours.
7) After cooking time is finished, uncover the slow cooker and serve hot with the garnishing of parsley.

Quinoa with Spinach

Cook time: 2¼ hours | Serves: 4 | Per Serving: Calories 267, Carbs 34.4g, Fat 10.5g, Protein 10g

Ingredients:

- Olive oil – 2 tbsp.
- Onion – 1, chopped
- Low-sodium vegetable broth – 2 C.
- Large tomatoes – 2, seeded and chopped
- Quinoa – 1 C. rinsed
- Salt and ground black pepper, as required
- Fresh baby spinach – 2 C.

Directions:

1) In a non-stick wok, heat oil over medium heat and sauté onion for about 4-5 minutes.
2) Add broth and tomatoes and bring to a boil.

3) Immediately transfer the tomato mixture into a slow cooker.
4) Add quinoa and black pepper and stir to combine.
5) Close the lid of the slow cooker and set on "Low" setting for 2 hours.
6) After cooking time is finished, uncover the slow cooker and stir in spinach.
7) Again, close the lid of slow cooker and set on "High" setting for 15 minutes.
8) After cooking time is finished, uncover the slow cooker and stir the mixture.
9) Serve hot.

Spiced Chickpeas

Cook time: 6 hours | Serves: 4 | Per Serving: Calories 410, Carbs 63g, Fat 15.4g, Protein 14.2g

Ingredients:

- Dried chickpeas – 6 oz. soaked overnight and drained
- Extra-virgin olive oil – ¼ C.
- Large onion – 1, chopped
- Crushed tomatoes – 1 (18-oz.) can
- Carrot – 1, peeled and chopped
- medium potatoes 2, chopped
- Garlic cloves – 2, minced
- Fresh cilantro ¼ C. chopped
- Ground turmeric – ½ tsp.
- Paprika – ½ tsp.
- Ground cumin – ½ tsp.
- Ground coriander – ¼ tsp.
- Ground cinnamon – ¼ tsp.
- Curry powder – ¼ tsp.
- Red pepper flakes – ¼ tsp. crushed
- Salt and ground black pepper, as required
- Honey – 1 tbsp.
- Water – 2¼ C.

Directions:

1) In the pot of a slow cooker, place all the ingredients and stir to combine.
2) Close the lid of slow cooker and set on "High" setting for 6 hours.
3) After cooking time is finished, uncover the slow cooker and serve hot.

Pasta with Asparagus

Cook time: 8 hours │ Serves: 4 │ Per Serving: Calories 396, Carbs 63.7g, Fat 9.4g, Protein 16.5g

Ingredients:

- Diced tomatoes with basil, oregano, and garlic – 3 (14½-oz.) cans
- Asparagus – 14 oz. trimmed and sliced
- Garlic cloves – 6, minced
- Whipping cream – ½ C.
- Dried penne pasta – 12 oz.
- Feta cheese – ¼ C. crumbled

Directions:

1) Grease the pot of a slow cooker.
2) Drain the juices from two cans of diced tomatoes.
3) In the prepared slow cooker, place the drained and undrained tomatoes alongside the asparagus and garlic and mix well.
4) Close the lid of slow cooker and set on "Low" setting for 6-8 hours.
5) Meanwhile, in a large pan of lightly salted boiling water, cook the pasta for about 8-10 minutes or according to the package's directions.
6) Drain the pasta and rinse under cold running water.
7) After cooking time is finished, uncover the slow cooker and stir in the whipping cream.
8) Divide the pasta onto serving plates and top with asparagus sauce.
9) Garnish with cheese and serve.

Veggie Lasagna

Cook time: 2 hours │ Serves: 4 │ Per Serving: Calories 313, Carbs 38.5g, Fat 8.8g, Protein 20.5g

Ingredients:

- Baby spinach – 3 oz. chopped roughly
- Large Portobello mushroom caps – 2, gills removed, halved and sliced thinly
- Small zucchini – ½. quartered lengthwise and sliced thinly
- Part-skim ricotta cheese – 8-oz.
- Medium egg – 1
- Diced tomatoes – 1 (14-oz.) can
- Crushed tomatoes – 1 (14-oz.) can
- Garlic cloves – 2, minced
- Red pepper flakes – ¼ tsp. crushed
- Uncooked whole-wheat lasagna noodles – 8
- Part-skim mozzarella cheese – 1½ C. shredded and divided

Directions:

1) Generously grease the pot of a slow cooker.
2) In a large-sized bowl, add spinach, zucchini, ricotta cheese and egg and mix well.
3) In another large-sized bowl, add both cans of tomatoes with juices, garlic and red pepper flakes and mix well.
4) In the bottom of the prepared slow cooker, place about 1½ C. of the tomato mixture evenly.
5) Place 5 lasagna noodles over the tomato mixture, overlapping them slightly and breaking them to fit in the pot.
6) Spread half of the ricotta mixture over the noodles.
7) Now, place about 1½ C. of the tomato mixture and sprinkle with 1 C. of the mozzarella.
8) Repeat the layers twice.
9) Close the lid of slow cooker and set on "High" setting for 2 hours.
10) After cooking time is finished, uncover the slow cooker and sprinkle with the remaining mozzarella cheese.
11) Immediately cover the slow cooker with lid for about 10 minutes before serving.

Salmon Risotto

Cook time: 1 hour 20 minutes | Serves: 4 | Per Serving: Calories 579, Carbs 53g, Fat 22.5g, Protein 34.1g

Ingredients:

- Olive oil – 2 tbsp.
- Shallots – 2, chopped
- Small cucumber – 1, peeled, seeded and chopped
- Arborio rice – 1¼ C. rinsed and drained
- Hot Low-sodium vegetable broth – 3 C.
- White wine – ½ C.
- Skinless, boneless salmon fillet – 1¼ lb. chopped
- Salt and ground black pepper, as required
- Scallion – 1, chopped
- Fresh dill – 3 tbsp. chopped

Directions:

1) In a pan, heat the oil over medium-high heat and sauté the shallot and cucumber for about 2-3 minutes.
2) Adjust the heat to low and cook, covered for about 15 minutes.
3) Add the rice and stir to combine.
4) Adjust the heat to high and sauté for about 1 minute.
5) Remove from the heat and transfer the rice mixture into a slow cooker.
6) Pour the hot broth and wine on top.
7) Close the lid of the slow cooker and set on "High" setting for 45 minutes.

8) After cooking time is finished, uncover the slow cooker and stir in the salmon pieces, salt and black pepper.
9) Close the lid of slow cooker and set on "High" setting for 15 minutes.
10) After cooking time is finished, switch off the Slow Cooker and let the risotto stand, covered for about 5 minutes.
11) After cooking time is finished, uncover the slow cooker and stir in the scallion and dill.
12) Serve hot.

Shrimp with Orzo

Cook time: 3 hours 16 minutes | Serves: 4 | Per Serving: Calories 499, Carbs 23g, Fat 27.8g, Protein 39.2g

Ingredients:

- Uncooked orzo pasta – ½ C.
- Dried basil – 2 tsp.
- Olive oil – 2 tbsp. divided
- Butter – 2 tbsp.
- Shallot – 1½ tbsp. chopped
- Diced tomatoes – 1 (14-oz.) can, drained
- Garlic cloves – 2, minced
- Dried oregano – 1 tsp.
- Shrimp – 1 lb. peeled and deveined
- Oil-packed sun-dried tomatoes – ¾ C. chopped
- Greek olives – 1 C. pitted
- Feta cheese – 2 C. crumbled

Directions:

1) Grease the pot of a slow cooker.
2) In a large pan of lightly salted boiling water, cook the orzo for about 8-10 minutes or according to the package's directions.
3) Drain the orzo and rinse under cold running water.
4) Transfer the orzo into a large-sized bowl with basil and 1 tbsp. of oil and toss to coat well. Set aside.
5) In a large-sized wok, heat the remaining oil and butter over medium heat and sauté the shallot for about 2-3 minutes.
6) Add the tomatoes, garlic and oregano and cook for about 1-2 minutes.
7) Add the shrimp and sun-dried tomatoes and cook for about 1 minute.
8) Remove from the heat and place the shrimp mixture into the prepared slow cooker.
9) Add the orzo mixture, olives and cheese and stir to combine.
10) Close the lid of slow cooker and set on "Low" setting for 2-3 hours.
11) After cooking time is finished, uncover the slow cooker and immediately stir in feta.
12) Serve hot.

Shrimp with Tomatoes

Cook time: 7¼ hours | Serves: 4 | Per Serving: Calories 248, Carbs 12.8g, Fat 3.3g, Protein 41.1g

Ingredients:

- Whole peeled tomatoes – 1 (14-oz.) can, finely chopped
- Canned tomato paste – 4 oz.
- Garlic cloves – 2, minced
- Fresh parsley – 2 tbsp. chopped
- Salt and ground black pepper, as required
- Lemon pepper – 1 tsp.
- Cooked shrimp – 1½ lb. peeled and deveined

Directions:

1) In the pot of a slow cooker, add all ingredients except for shrimp and stir to combine.
2) Close the lid of slow cooker and set on "Low" setting for 6-7 hours.
3) After cooking time is finished, uncover the slow cooker and stir in the shrimp.
4) Again, close the lid of slow cooker and set on "High" setting for 15 minutes.
5) After cooking time is finished, uncover the slow cooker and serve hot.

Pork Meatballs

Cook time: 6 hours 10 minutes | Serves: 4 | Per Serving: Calories 497, Carbs 14.4g, Fat 38.8g, Protein 27.2g

Ingredients:

For Meatballs:

- Lean ground pork – 1 lb.
- Onion – 1/3 C. finely chopped and divided
- Fresh parsley – 2 tbsp. chopped
- Whole-wheat dried breadcrumbs – 2½ tbsp.
- Large egg – 1, beaten lightly
- Ground cumin – ½ tsp.
- Smoked paprika – ½ tsp.
- Ground black pepper, as required
- Extra-virgin olive oil – 2 tbsp
- Diced tomatoes – 1 (15-oz.) can
- Salt, as required

For Salad:

- Fresh mixed salad greens – 6 C.
- Walnuts – ¼ C.
- Extra-virgin olive oil – 2 tbsp.
- Fresh lemon juice – 1 tbsp.

Directions:

1) In a large-sized bowl, add pork, 1/3 of C. onion, parsley, breadcrumbs, eggs, cumin, ¼ tsp. of paprika, and black pepper and mix well until blended.
2) Make desired size balls from mixture.
3) In a large-sized non-stick wok, heat oil over medium-high heat and cook the meatballs for about 4-6 minutes.
4) With a slotted spoon, transfer meatballs into a slow cooker.
5) In the same wok, add remaining onion and sauté for about 3-4 minutes.
6) Place onion over meatballs in the slow cooker, followed by reminding ¼ tsp paprika, tomatoes and a little salt.
7) Close the lid of slow cooker and set on "Low" setting for 5-6 hours.
8) After cooking time is finished, uncover the slow cooker and serve hot.

Snacks & Appetizer Recipes

Herbed Almonds

Cook time: 1½ hours | Serves: 4 | Per Serving: Calories 155, Carbs 5.6g, Fat 13.7g, Protein 5.1g

Ingredients:

- Raw almonds – 1 C.
- Olive oil – ½ tbsp.
- Dried rosemary – ½ tbsp.
- Dried thyme – ½ tbsp.
- Salt and ground black pepper, as required

Directions:

1) In the pot of a slow cooker, add all ingredients and stir to combine
2) Close the lid of slow cooker and set on "High" setting for 1½ hours.
3) While cooking, stir the almonds after every 30 minutes.
4) After cooking time is finished, uncover the slow cooker and transfer the almonds into a heatproof bowl.
5) Set aside to cool before serving.

Sweet Cinnamon Walnuts

Cook time: 2 hours 40 minutes | Serves: 4 | Per Serving: Calories 114, Carbs 5.4g, Fat 10.3g, Protein 1.2g

Ingredients:

- Unsalted butter – 2 tbsp.
- Raw walnuts – 1 C.
- Ground cinnamon – 1 tsp.
- Powdered sugar – 2-3 tbsp.

Directions:

1) In a non-stick wok, melt butter over medium-low heat and cook the walnuts for about 10 minutes, stirring frequently.
2) Immediately transfer the walnuts into the slow cooker.
3) Add the cinnamon and sugar and stir to combine.

4) Close the lid of the slow cooker and set on "High" setting for 2-2½ hours.
5) After cooking time is finished, uncover the slow cooker and transfer the walnuts into a heatproof bowl.
6) Set aside to cool before serving.

BBQ Chicken Wings

Cook time: 7¼ hours | Serves: 4 | Per Serving: Calories 477, Carbs 12g, Fat 12.7g, Protein 49.2g

Ingredients:

- BBQ sauce – ½ C.
- Chicken wings – 1½ lb.
- Arrowroot starch – 3 tsp.
- Water – 1 tbsp.

Directions:

1) In the pot of a slow cooker, place the chicken wings and top with the BBQ sauce evenly.
2) Close the lid of slow cooker and set on "Low" setting for 6-7 hours.
3) Meanwhile, in a small-sized bowl, dissolve the arrowroot starch in water.
4) After cooking time is finished, uncover the slow cooker.
5) In the pot, add the arrowroot starch mixture, stirring continuously until well blended.
6) Close the lid of slow cooker and set on "High" setting for 12-15 minutes.
7) After cooking time is finished, uncover the slow cooker and serve immediately.

Sausage Poppers

Cook time: 4 hours | Serves: 4 | Per Serving: Calories 298, Carbs 2.7g, Fat 24.6g, Protein 14.2g

Ingredients:

- Low-fat cream cheese – 4 oz. softened
- Sharp cheddar cheese 1/3 C. shredded
- Light sour cream – 3 tbsp.
- Cooked bacon strips – 4, crumbled
- Jalapeño peppers – 4, cut in half and seeded

Directions:

1) In a medium-sized mixing bowl, stir together the cream cheese, cheddar cheese, sour cream and bacon.
2) Stuff each bell pepper half with bacon mixture evenly.
3) In the pot of a slow cooker, place about 1/3 C. of water.
4) Arrange the stuffed peppers in the slow cooker in a single layer.
5) Close the lid of slow cooker and set on "Low" setting for 4 hours.
6) After cooking time is finished, uncover the slow cooker and serve hot.

BBQ Little Smokies

Cook time: 2 hours | Serves: 4 | Per Serving: Calories 472, Carbs 41.4g, Fat 27.7g, Protein 17.3g

Ingredients:

- Tomato ketchup – 1 C.
- Powdered sugar – ¾ C.
- Onion – ¼ C. minced
- Liquid smoke – 1 tbsp.
- Cocktail sausages – 1 (13-oz.) package

Directions:

1) In the pot of a slow cooker, place all ingredients except for the sausages and mix well.
2) Add the sausages and stir to combine.
3) Close the lid of slow cooker and set on "High" setting for 2 hours.
4) After cooking time is finished, uncover the slow cooker and transfer the sausages onto a platter.
5) Serve immediately.

Eggplant Tapenade

Cook time: 9 hours | Serves: 4 | Per Serving: Calories 44, Carbs 9.8g, Fat 0.4g, Protein 2g

Ingredients:

- Eggplants 4 C. chopped
- Tomatoes – 2 C. chopped
- Garlic cloves – 5-6, minced
- Capers – 4 tsp.
- Fresh lemon juice – 4 tsp.
- Dried basil – 2 tsp.
- Salt and ground black pepper, as required

Directions:

1) In the pot of a slow cooker, add eggplant, tomatoes, garlic and capers and mix well.
2) Close the lid of slow cooker and set on "Low" setting for 7-9 hours.
3) After cooking time is finished, uncover the slow cooker and stir in the remaining ingredients.
4) Serve hot.

Chickpea Hummus

Cook time: 4 hours | Serves: 4 | Per Serving: Calories 189, Carbs 10.6g, Fat 17.7g, Protein 6.6g

Ingredients:

- Dried chickpeas – ¾ C. rinsed
- Water – 2 C.
- Garlic clove – 1, peeled
- Olive oil – 3 tbsp. divided
- Fresh lemon juice – 1 tbsp.
- Tahini – 2 tbsp.
- Fresh parsley, 2 tbsp. chopped

Directions:

1) In the pot of a slow cooker, place the chickpeas and water.
2) Close the lid of slow cooker and set on "High" setting for 4 hours.
3) After cooking time is finished, uncover the slow cooker and drain the chickpeas, reserving about 1/3 C. of the cooking liquid.
4) In a clean food processor, add chickpeas, reserved cooking liquid, garlic, 2 tbsp. of oil, lemon juice and tahini and pulse until smooth.
5) Transfer the hummus into a bowl and refrigerator before serving.
6) Just before serving, drizzle the hummus with remaining oil and garnish with parsley.

Taco Cheese Dip

Cook time: 1 hour 20 minutes | Serves: 4 | Per Serving: Calories 171, Carbs 7.9g, Fat 12.2g, Protein 10.5g

Ingredients:

- Velveeta cheese – 8 oz. cubed
- Canned diced tomatoes with green chile peppers – ¾ C.
- Taco seasoning – 1 tsp.

Directions:

1) In the pot of a slow cooker, place the Velveeta cheese cubes.
2) Close the lid of slow cooker and set on "Low" setting for 50 minutes.
3) During cooking, stir the cheese occasionally.
4) After cooking time is finished, uncover the slow cooker and stir in the tomatoes and taco seasoning.
5) Again, close the lid of slow cooker and set on "Low" setting for 30 minutes
6) After cooking time is finished, uncover the slow cooker and stir well.
7) Serve warm.

Artichoke & Spinach Dip

Cook time: 7¼ hours | Serves: 4 | Per Serving: Calories 182, Carbs 10g, Fat 12.3g, Protein 9.5g

Ingredients:

- Canned quartered artichoke hearts – 6 oz. chopped and drained
- Fresh baby spinach – 5 oz. roughly chopped
- Low-fat cream cheese – 4 oz. cubed
- Plain Greek yogurt – ½ C.
- Mozzarella cheese – ½ C. shredded
- Parmesan cheese – ¼ C. grated
- Red onion – 3 tbsp. finely chopped
- Garlic cloves – 2, minced
- Ground black pepper – ½ tsp.

Directions:

1) In the pot of a slow cooker, add all ingredients and gently stir to combine.
2) Close the lid of slow cooker and set on "Low" setting for 2-3 hours.
3) After cooking time is finished, uncover the slow cooker and stir well.
4) Serve warm.

Cheese Fondue

Cook time: 3 hours 10 minutes | Serves: 4 | Per Serving: Calories 527, Carbs 6.5g, Fat 39.7g, Protein 34.6g

Ingredients:

- Garlic clove – 1, cut in half
- Chicken broth – 2 C.
- Fresh lemon juice – 2 tbsp.
- Swiss cheese – 12 oz. shredded
- Cheddar cheese – 6 oz. shredded
- Almond flour – 2 tbsp.
- Pinch of ground nutmeg
- Pinch of paprika
- Pinch of ground black pepper

Directions:

1) Rub a pan with cut garlic halves evenly.
2) Add broth and place pan over medium heat.
3) Cook until it is just beginning to bubble.
4) Now adjust heat to low and stir in lemon juice.
5) Meanwhile, in a bowl, blend together both cheeses and flour.
6) Slowly add cheese mixture, stirring continuously.
7) Cook for about 2-3 minutes or until cheese mixture becomes thick, stirring continuously.
8) Grease the pot of a slow cooker.
9) Transfer the cheese mixture into the greased pot of slow cooker and sprinkle with nutmeg, paprika and black pepper.
10) Close the lid of slow cooker and set on "Low" setting for 3 hours.
11) After cooking time is finished, uncover the slow cooker and stir well.
12) Serve hot.

Soup Recipes

Onion Soup

Cook time: 5 hours 10 minutes | Serves: 4 | Per Serving: Calories 124, Carbs 8.1g, Fat 8.3g, Protein 5.8g

Ingredients:

- Olive oil – 2 tbsp.
- Medium sweet onions – 2, sliced
- Garlic cloves 2, minced
- Low-sodium soy sauce – ¼ C.
- Unsweetened applesauce – 1 tsp.
- Dried oregano – 1 tsp. crushed
- Dried basil – 1 tsp. crushed
- Ground black pepper, as required
- Low-sodium vegetable broth – 4 C.
- Parmesan cheese – ¼ C. grated

Directions:

1) In a non-stick saucepan, heat the oil over medium-low heat and cook the onion for about 8-9 minutes, stirring occasionally.
2) Add the garlic and cook for about 1 minute.
3) Immediately transfer the onion mixture into a slow cooker.
4) Add the remaining ingredients except for cheese and stir to combine.
5) Close the lid of slow cooker and set on "Low" setting for 4-5 hours.
6) After cooking time is finished, uncover the slow cooker and stir in the cheese until melted completely.
7) Serve hot.

Broccoli Soup

Cook time: 6 hours 10 minutes | Serves: 4 | Per Serving: Calories 167, Carbs 10.4g, Fat 12.2g, Protein 5.3g

Ingredients:

- Unsalted butter – 2 tbsp.
- Onion – 1, chopped
- Garlic cloves – 2, minced
- Fresh rosemary – 1 tbsp. chopped
- Small broccoli florets – 3 C.
- Low-sodium vegetable broth – 4 C.
- Salt and ground black pepper, as required
- Light sour cream – ½ C.

Directions:

1) In a non-stick wok, melt butter over medium heat and sauté onion for about 3-4 minutes.
2) Add garlic and rosemary and sauté for about 1 minute.
3) Transfer the onion mixture into a slow cooker.
4) Add broccoli, broth, salt and black pepper and stir to combine.
5) Close the lid of slow cooker and set on "Low" setting for 6 hours.
6) After cooking time is finished, uncover the slow cooker and let the soup cool slightly.
7) Transfer the soup into a blender in batches and pulse until smooth.
8) Transfer the soup into a large pan over medium heat.
9) Stir in cream and cook for about 4-5 minutes.
10) Serve hot.

Squash & Apple Soup

Cook time: 8 hours | Serves: 4 | Per Serving: Calories 237, Carbs 37.5g, Fat 8.7g, Protein 4.3g

Ingredients:

- Butternut squash – 4 C. peeled and chopped
- Medium Granny Smith apples – 2, peeled, cored and chopped
- Small carrot – 1, peeled and chopped
- Small white onion – 1, chopped
- Garlic clove – 1, minced
- Low-sodium chicken broth – 3 C.
- Dried oregano – 1 tsp. crushed
- Dried thyme – 1 tsp. crushed
- Salt and ground black pepper, as required
- Unsweetened coconut milk – 1 C.

Directions:

1) In the pot of a slow cooker, add all ingredients except for coconut milk and stir to combine.
2) Close the lid of slow cooker and set on "Low" setting for 6-8 hours.
3) After cooking time is finished, uncover the slow cooker and stir in the coconut milk.
4) With a stick blender, puree the soup until smooth.
5) Serve immediately.

Mixed Veggies Soup

Cook time: 8 hours 5 minutes │Serves: 4 │ Per Serving: Calories 91, Carbs 11.1g, Fat 3.9g, Protein 4.3g

Ingredients:

- Olive oil – 1 tbsp.
- Onion – 1, chopped
- Celery stalk – 1, chopped
- Small carrot – 1, peeled and chopped
- Garlic cloves – 2, minced
- Dried oregano – 1 tsp. crushed
- Large zucchini – 1, chopped
- Tomatoes – 2, chopped
- Fresh spinach 1 C. chopped
- Low-sodium vegetable broth – 4 C.
- Salt and ground black pepper, as required

Directions:

1) In a pan, heat the oil over medium heat and sauté the onion, celery and carrot for about 3-4 minutes.
2) Add the garlic and thyme and sauté for about 1 minute.
3) Transfer the onion mixture into a slow cooker.
4) Add remaining ingredients and stir to combine.
5) Close the lid of slow cooker and set on "Low" setting for 8 hours.
6) After cooking time is finished, uncover the slow cooker and serve hot.

Lentil & Veggie Soup

Cook time: 8 hours 35 minutes │Serves: 4 │ Per Serving: Calories 343, Carbs 49g, Fat 8.2g, Protein 20.5g

Ingredients:

- Olive oil – 2 tbsp.
- Onions – 1 C. finely chopped
- Celery stalk – 1 C. finely chopped
- Garlic cloves – 2, minced
- Ground coriander ½ tsp.
- Ground cumin – ½ tsp.
- Ground turmeric – ½ tsp.
- Salt and ground black pepper, as required
- Cauliflower – 1 C. chopped
- Diced tomatoes – 1 (14-oz.) can
- Lentils – 1¼ C. rinsed
- Tomato paste – 2 tbsp.
- Low-sodium vegetable broth – 4 C.
- Fresh spinach – 3 C. chopped

Directions:

1) In a pan, heat the oil over medium heat and sauté the onion and celery for about 3-4 minutes.
2) Add the garlic and spices and cook for about 1 minute.
3) Transfer the onion mixture into a slow cooker.
4) Add remaining ingredients except for spinach and stir to combine.
5) Close the lid of the slow cooker and set on "Low" setting for 8-8½ hours.
6) After cooking time is finished, uncover the slow cooker and stir in the spinach.
7) Again, close the lid of the slow cooker and set on "Low" setting for 30 minutes.
8) After cooking time is finished, uncover the slow cooker and serve hot.

Chicken & Bean Soup

Cook time: 4 hours ┃Serves: 4 ┃ Per Serving: Calories 273, Carbs 31.6g, Fat 10g, Protein 38.6g

Ingredients:

- Cooked chicken – 1 lb. shredded
- Great Northern beans – 1½ (15-oz.) cans, drained and rinsed
- Carrots – 2, peeled and chopped
- Celery stalks – 2, chopped
- Fresh baby spinach – 4 C.
- Onion – 1, chopped
- Garlic cloves – 2, minced
- Bay leaf – 1
- Salt and ground black pepper, as required
- Low-sodium chicken broth – 4¼ C.

Directions:

1) In the pot of a slow cooker, place all the ingredients and stir to combine.
2) Close the lid of the slow cooker and set on "High" setting for 3-4 hours.
3) After cooking time is finished, uncover the slow cooker and serve hot.

Meatballs, Chickpeas & Pasta Soup

Cook time: 4½ hours | Serves: 4 | Per Serving: Calories 614, Carbs 10.6g, Fat 68.7g, Protein 37.4g

Ingredients:

- Frozen turkey meatballs – 12-16
- Chickpeas – 1 (14-oz.) can, drained and rinsed
- Medium carrots – 2, peeled and chopped
- Medium onion – 1, chopped
- Fire-roasted diced tomatoes – 1 (28-oz.) can
- Garlic clove – 1, minced
- Lemon zest – 1 tbsp. grated
- Low-sodium chicken broth – 4 C.
- Tomato sauce – 1 (8-oz.) can
- Dried oregano – ½ tsp.
- Dried parsley – ½ tsp.
- Salt and ground black pepper, as required
- Fresh baby spinach leaves – 2-3 C.
- Orzo – 1 C.

Directions:

1) In the pot of a slow cooker, place all the ingredients except for spinach and orzo and stir to combine.
2) Close the lid of slow cooker and set on "High" setting for 3-4 hours.
3) After cooking time is finished, uncover the slow cooker and stir in the spinach and orzo.
4) Again, close the lid of slow cooker and set on "High" setting for 20-30 minutes.
5) After cooking time is finished, uncover the slow cooker and serve hot.

Cheesy Beef Soup

Cook time: 5 hours 40 minutes | Serves: 4 | Per Serving: Calories 445, Carbs 5.8g, Fat 27.7g, Protein 41.2g

Ingredients:

- Unsalted butter – 2 tbsp.
- Medium onion – 1, chopped
- Celery stalk – 1, chopped
- Garlic cloves – 2, minced
- Cooked beef – 1 lb. chopped
- Low-sodium beef broth – 4 C.
- Salt and ground black pepper, as required
- Heavy cream – 1 C.
- Swiss cheese – ½ C. shredded

Directions:

1) In a pan, melt butter over medium heat and sauté the onion, celery and garlic for about 4-5 minutes.
2) Transfer the onion mixture into a slow cooker.
3) Add beef, broth, salt and black pepper and stir to combine.
4) Close the lid of slow cooker and set on "High" setting for 4½ hours.
5) After cooking time is finished, uncover the slow cooker and stir in the heavy cream and cheese.
6) Again, close the lid of slow cooker and set on "High" setting for 1 hour.
7) After cooking time is finished, uncover the slow cooker and serve hot.

Sausage & Beans Soup

Cook time: 6 hours | Serves: 4 | Per Serving: Calories 424, Carbs 47.1g, Fat 12.1g, Protein 33g

Ingredients:

- Smoked sausage – 1 lb. sliced
- Mixed dry beans – ½ lb. rinsed, soaked overnight and drained
- Onion – 1, chopped
- Garlic clove – 1, minced
- Diced tomatoes with liquid – 1 (18-oz.) can
- Low-sodium chicken broth – 4 C.
- Salt and ground black pepper, as required
- Fresh spinach – 2-3 C.

Directions:

1) In the pot of a slow cooker, add all ingredients except for spinach and stir to combine.
2) Close the lid of slow cooker and set on "High" setting for 5½ hours.
3) After cooking time is finished, uncover the slow cooker and stir in spinach.
4) Close the lid of slow cooker and set on "High" setting for 30 minutes.
5) After cooking time is finished, uncover the slow cooker and serve hot.

Shrimp Soup

Cook time: 5 hours | Serves: 4 | Per Serving: Calories 243, Carbs 17.6g, Fat 3.3g, Protein 30g

Ingredients:

- Onion – 1, chopped
- Small bell pepper – 1, seeded and chopped
- Diced tomatoes with juices – 1 (14-oz.) can
- Canned mushrooms – 2 oz.
- Black olives – ¼ C. pitted and sliced
- Garlic cloves – 2, minced
- Tomato sauce – 1 (6-oz.) can
- Bay leaves – 2
- Dried basil – 1 tsp.
- Salt and ground black pepper, as required
- Dry white wine – ½ C.
- Fresh orange juice – ½ C.
- Low-sodium chicken broth – 24 fluid oz.
- Medium shrimp – 1 lb. peeled and deveined

Directions:

1) In the pot of a slow cooker, place all the ingredients except for shrimp and stir to combine.
2) Close the lid of slow cooker and set on "Low" setting for 4-4½ hours.
3) After cooking time is finished, uncover the slow cooker and stir in the shrimp.
4) Close the lid of slow cooker and set on "Low" setting for 20-30 minutes.
5) After cooking time is finished, uncover the slow cooker and discard the bay leaves.
6) Serve hot.

Stew & Chili Recipes

Turkey & Spinach Stew

Cook time: 6 hours 10 minutes | Serves: 4 | Per Serving: Calories 239, Carbs 7.5g, Fat 8g, Protein 37.9g

Ingredients:

- Olive oil – 2 tbsp. divided
- Boneless turkey breast – 1¼ lb. cubed
- Garlic powder – 1 tsp.
- Salt and ground black pepper, as required
- Small onion – 1, chopped
- Dried thyme – ½ tsp. crushed
- Dried oregano – ½ tsp. crushed
- Carrot – ½ C. peeled and chopped
- Celery stalk – 1, chopped
- Fresh spinach – 5 C. chopped
- Tomatoes – 1 C. finely chopped
- Low-sodium chicken broth – 1½ C.
- Fresh lemon juice – 2 tbsp.

Directions:

1) In a non-stick pan, heat 1 tbsp. of the oil over medium heat and cook the turkey cubes with garlic powder, salt and black pepper for about 4-5 minutes.
2) With a slotted spoon, transfer the turkey cubes into a slow cooker.
3) In the pan, add the remaining oil and onions and cook for about 4-5 minutes.
4) Transfer the onion into the pot of slow cooker.
5) Add remaining ingredients except for lemon juice and stir to combine
6) Close the lid of slow cooker and set on "Low" setting for 6 hours.
7) After cooking time is finished, uncover the slow cooker and stir in the lemon juice.
8) Serve hot.

Beef & Carrot Stew

Cook time: 9 hours | Serves: 4 | Per Serving: Calories 269, Carbs 12.6g, Fat 7.3g, Protein 36.5g

Ingredients:

- Beef stew meat – 1 lb. trimmed and cubed
- Salt and ground black pepper, as required
- Carrots – 2½ C. peeled and sliced
- Medium onion – 1, chopped
- Garlic cloves – 3, minced
- Medium tomatoes – 2, chopped
- Low-sodium beef broth – 1 C.
- Fresh parsley – 2 tbsp. chopped

Directions:

1) In the pot of a slow cooker, add all ingredients except for parsley and mix well.
2) Close the lid of slow cooker and set on "Low" setting for 9 hours.
3) After cooking time is finished, uncover the slow cooker and serve hot with the garnishing of parsley.

Spicy Lamb & Olive Stew

Cook time: 8¾ hours | Serves: 4 | Per Serving: Calories 421, Carbs 11.1g, Fat 23.8g, Protein 39.6g

Ingredients:

- Olive oil – 2 tbsp.
- 1¼ lb. lamb shoulder, cubed
- Onion – 1, sliced
- Garlic cloves – 3, crushed
- Fresh ginger – 1 tsp. grated
- Ground cumin – 1 tsp.
- Ground coriander – 1 tsp.
- Pinch of saffron
- Lemon peel – 1 tsp. grated
- Tomato puree – 1 tbsp.
- Hot Low-sodium beef broth – 2 C.
- Salt and ground black pepper, as required
- Kalamata olives – ¾ C. pitted
- Honey – 1 tbsp.
- Fresh lemon juice – 2 tbsp.

Directions:

1) In a large-sized wok, heat 1 tbsp. of the oil over medium-high heat and cook the lamb cubes for about 4-5 minutes or until browned completely.
2) With a slotted spoon, transfer the lamb cubes into a slow cooker.
3) In the same wok, heat the remaining oil over medium heat and sauté the onion for about 4-6 minutes.
4) Add the garlic and ginger and sauté for about 1-2 minutes.
5) Add the spices, saffron, lemon peel and tomato puree and sauté for about 1-2 minutes.
6) Transfer the onion mixture into the slow cooker with broth, salt and black pepper and stir to combine.
7) Close the lid of the slow cooker and set on "Low" setting for 6-8 hours.
8) After cooking time is finished, uncover the slow cooker and stir in the olives, honey and lemon juice.
9) Again, close the lid of the slow cooker and set on "High" setting for 20-30 minutes.
10) After cooking time is finished, uncover the slow cooker and serve hot.

Pork & Cabbage Stew

Cook time: 7½ hours | Serves: 4 | Per Serving: Calories 240, Carbs 6.4g, Fat 8g, Protein 39.2g

Ingredients:

- Boneless country-style pork ribs – 1¼ lb.
- Cabbage – 1¼ C. chopped
- Tomatoes – ¼ C. finely chopped
- Small onion – 1, chopped
- Garlic cloves – 2, minced
- Olive oil – 2 tbsp.
- Low-sodium chicken broth – 2 C.
- Fresh oregano – 1 tbsp. minced
- Salt and ground black pepper, as required
- Fresh lime juice – 2 tbsp.

Directions:

1) In the pot of a slow cooker, add all ingredients and mix well.
2) Close the lid of slow cooker and set on "Low" setting for 7½ hours.
3) After cooking time is finished, uncover the slow cooker and transfer pork into large-sized bowl.
4) With 2 forks, shred the meat.
5) Return the shredded pork into the pot and mix well.
6) Serve hot with the drizzling of lime juice.

Herbed Seafood Stew

Cook time: 4¾ hours | Serves: 4 | Per Serving: Calories 255, Carbs 7.2g, Fat 9.2g, Protein 34.9g

Ingredients:

- Celery stalk – 1, chopped
- Small yellow onion – 1, chopped
- Garlic cloves – 2, chopped
- Fresh cilantro leaves – ½ C. chopped
- Tomatoes 1 C. finely chopped
- Low-sodium chicken broth – 2 C.
- Fresh lemon juice – 2 tbsp.
- Olive oil – 2 tbsp.
- Mixed dried herbs – 2 tsp.
- Salt and ground black pepper, as required
- Cod fillets – ½ lb. cubed
- Shrimp – ½ lb. peeled and deveined
- Scallops – ½ lb.
- Crabmeat – ½ C.

Directions:

1) In the pot of a slow cooker, add all ingredients except for seafood and mix well.
2) Close the lid of slow cooker and set on "High" setting for 4 hours.
3) After cooking time is finished, uncover the slow cooker and stir in seafood.
4) Now, close the lid of slow cooker and set on "Low" setting for 30-45 minutes.
5) After cooking time is finished, uncover the slow cooker and serve hot.

Beans Chili

Cook time: 8 hours | Serves: 4 | Per Serving: Calories 344, Carbs 65.8g, Fat 2.3g, Protein 19.8g

Ingredients:

- Bell pepper – 1, seeded and chopped
- Medium onion – 1, chopped
- 4 Garlic cloves, minced
- Medium sweet potato – 1, peeled and cubed
- Diced tomatoes with juices – 1 (28-oz.) can
- Red kidney beans – 1 (15½-oz.) can, rinsed and drained
- Black beans – 1 (15½-oz.) can, rinsed and drained
- Unsweetened cocoa powder – 2 tbsp.
- Red chili powder – 2 tbsp.
- Ground cumin – 1 tbsp.
- Salt and ground black pepper, as required
- Low-sodium vegetable broth – 1 C.
- Fresh cilantro 2 tbsp. chopped

Directions:

1) In the pot of a slow cooker add all ingredients except for cilantro and stir to combine.
2) Close the lid of slow cooker and set on "Low" setting for 7-8 hours.
3) After cooking time is finished, uncover the slow cooker and serve hot. Add the garnishing of cilantro.

Beans & Quinoa Chili

Cook time: 6 hours 6 minutes | Serves: 4 | Per Serving: Calories 428, Carbs 67.3g, Fat 11.6g, Protein 17.7g

Ingredients:

- Olive oil – 2 tsp.
- Medium yellow onion – 1, chopped
- Celery stalks – 2, chopped
- Garlic cloves – 2, chopped
- Water – ¼ C.
- Tomato paste – 2 tbsp.
- Chipotle in adobo – 1½ tbsp. finely chopped
- Red chili powder – 2 tsp.
- Ground coriander 1 tsp.
- Ground cumin – 1 tsp.
- Ground cinnamon – ½ tsp.
- Smoked paprika – ½ tsp.
- Low-sodium vegetable broth – 2 C.
- Canned black beans – 2 C.
- Uncooked quinoa – 1 C. rinsed
- Butternut squash – ½ lb. peeled and cubed
- Fire-roasted, diced tomatoes with juices – 1 (14-oz.) can
- Small avocado – 1, peeled, pitted and sliced

Directions:

1) In a pan, heat the oil over a medium heat and sauté the onion and celery for about 3-4 minutes.
2) Add the garlic and sauté for about 1 minute.
3) Add the water, tomato paste, chipotle and spices and cook for about 1 minute, stirring continuously.
4) Transfer the onion mixture into a slow cooker.
5) Add the broth, black beans, quinoa, squash and tomatoes and stir to combine.
6) Close the lid of slow cooker and set on "Low" setting for 6 hours.
7) After cooking time is finished, uncover the slow cooker and serve hot with the topping of avocado slices.

Turkey & Beans Chili

Cook time: 5 hours 10 minutes | Serves: 4 | Per Serving: Calories 389, Carbs 43g, Fat 9.6g, Protein 35.9g

Ingredients:

- Lean ground turkey – 1 lb.
- Bell pepper – 1, seeded and chopped
- Red onion – 1, finely chopped
- Garlic cloves – 2, minced
- Tomatoes – 1½ C. finely chopped
- Canned black beans – 1½ C. rinsed and drained
- Canned red kidney beans – 1½ C. rinsed and drained
- Tomato paste – ¼ C.
- Red chili powder – 1 tbsp.
- Ground cumin – 1 tsp.
- Garlic powder – ½ tsp.
- Salt and ground black pepper, as required
- Low-sodium chicken broth – 1 C.
- Scallions – 2, chopped

Directions:

1) In a non-stick wok, heat oil over medium heat and cook the turkey for about 4-5 minutes.
2) Add bell pepper, onion and garlic and cook for about 4-5 minutes.
3) Remove the excess grease and transfer the turkey mixture into a slow cooker.
4) Add the remaining ingredients except for scallions and stir to combine.
5) Close the lid of the slow cooker and set on "Low" setting for 4-5 hours.
6) After cooking time is finished, uncover the slow cooker and serve hot with the topping of scallions.

Beef & Mushroom Chili

Cook time: 8 hours 10 minutes | Serves: 4 | Per Serving: Calories 322, Carbs 16g, Fat 11.9g, Protein 39.3g

Ingredients:

- Olive oil – 1 tbsp.
- Lean ground beef – 1 lb.
- Medium onion – 1, finely chopped
- Medium bell pepper – 1, seeded and chopped
- Fresh mushrooms – 8 oz. sliced
- Garlic cloves – 3, minced
- Jalapeño pepper – 1, seeded and chopped
- Diced tomatoes with juices – 1½ (14-oz.) cans

- Red chili powder – 2 tbsp.
- Cayenne pepper – 1 tsp.
- Salt and ground black pepper, as required
- Low-sodium beef broth – 1 C.
- Cheddar cheese – ¼ C. shredded

Directions:

1) In a non-stick wok, heat oil over a medium heat and cook the ground beef for about 4-5 minutes.
2) With a slotted spoon, transfer the ground beef into a slow cooker.
3) In the wok, add the onion, bell pepper, mushrooms and garlic and sauté for about 5 minutes.
4) Transfer the onion mixture into the slow cooker.
5) Add the remaining ingredients except for cheese and stir to combine.
6) Close the lid of slow cooker and set on "Low" setting for 8 hours.
7) After cooking time is finished, uncover the slow cooker and serve hot with the garnishing of cheese.

Pork, Beans & Corn Chili

Cook time: 7 hours 5 minutes │Serves: 4 │ Per Serving: Calories 458, Carbs 46.4g, Fat 12.2g, Protein 43.6g

Ingredients:

- Olive oil – 1 tbsp.
- Boneless pork – 1 lb. trimmed and cubed
- Salt and ground black pepper, as required
- Black beans – 1 (14-oz.) can, rinsed and drained
- Frozen corn – 1 C.
- Onion – 1 C. chopped
- Chopped green chiles – 2 oz.
- Crushed tomatoes – 1 (14-oz.) can
- Red chili powder – 2 tsp.
- Ground cumin – 1 tsp.
- Cayenne pepper – ½ tsp.
- Low-sodium chicken broth – 1 C.
- Light sour cream – ¼ C.

Directions:

1) In a non-stick wok, heat oil over a medium heat and cook the pork cubes with salt and black pepper for about 4-5 minutes.
2) Transfer the pork into a slow cooker.
3) Add the remaining ingredients except for sour cream and stir to combine.
4) Close the lid of the slow cooker and set on "Low" setting for 7 hours.

5) After cooking time is finished, uncover the slow cooker and serve hot with the topping of sour cream.

Chicken Recipes

Spiced Chicken Breasts

Cook time: 4 hours | Serves: 4 | Per Serving: Calories 220, Carbs 0.7g, Fat 8.5g, Protein 33.2g

Ingredients:

- Dried rosemary – ½ tsp.
- Ground cumin – ½ tsp.
- Paprika – ½ tsp.
- Cayenne pepper – ¼ tsp.
- Garlic powder – ¼ tsp.
- Onion powder – ¼ tsp.
- Salt and ground black pepper, as required
- Boneless, skinless chicken breasts – 4 (4-oz.)
- Low-sodium chicken broth – ½ C.

Directions:

1) In a small-sized bowl, blend together the rosemary, spices, salt and black pepper.
2) In the pot of a slow cooker, place the broth.
3) Arrange the chicken breasts in a single layer and sprinkle with spice mixture evenly.
4) Close the lid of the slow cooker and set on "High" setting for 3-4 hours.
5) After cooking time is finished, uncover the slow cooker and serve hot.

Garlicky Chicken Thighs

Cook time: 6 hours | Serves: 4 | Per Serving: Calories 293, Carbs 1g, Fat 14.7g, Protein 38.3g

Ingredients:

- Skinless, boneless chicken thighs – 4 (6-oz.)
- Unsalted butter – 3 tbsp. chopped
- Garlic cloves – 4, finely chopped
- Dried rosemary – 1 tbsp.
- Lemon pepper – 1 tsp.
- Salt and ground black pepper, as required

Directions:

1) In the pot of a slow cooker, place chicken thighs.
2) Top chicken thighs with butter evenly.
3) Sprinkle with garlic, rosemary, lemon pepper and black pepper evenly.
4) Close the lid of the slow cooker and set on "Low" setting for 6 hours.
5) After cooking time is finished, uncover the slow cooker and serve hot.

Glazed Chicken Thighs

Cook time: 5 hours | Serves: 4 | Per Serving: Calories 294, Carbs 19.6g, Fat 8.5g, Protein 34.3g

Good

Ingredients:

- Boneless, skinless chicken thighs – 4 (4-oz.)
- Low-sodium soy sauce – ¼ C.
- Maple syrup – ¼ C.
- Tomato ketchup – ¼ C.
- Sriracha – 2 tsp.
- Garlic cloves – 4, minced
- Dried oregano – ½ tsp.
- Dried parsley – ½ tsp.

Worschire Saue

Directions:

1) In a small-sized bowl, add all ingredients except for chicken thighs and beat until blended well.
2) Arrange the chicken thighs in the pot of a slow cooker in a single layer and top with ketchup mixture evenly.
3) Close the lid of the slow cooker and set on "Low" setting for 5 hours.
4) After cooking time is finished, uncover the slow cooker and serve hot.

BBQ Chicken Drumsticks

Cook time: 6 hours 5 minutes | Serves: 4 | Per Serving: Calories 464, Carbs 45.3g, Fat 14.2g, Protein 33.5g

Ingredients:

- Chicken drumsticks – 4 (8-oz.)
- BBQ spice rub – 2 tbsp.
- BBQ sauce – 2 C. divided

Directions:

1) Grease the pot of a slow cooker.
2) Rub each drumstick with spice rub generously.
3) In the pot of a slow cooker, place the drumsticks and 1½ C. of BBQ sauce and stir to combine.
4) Then arrange the drumsticks in a single layer.
5) Close the lid of slow cooker and set on "Low" setting for 6 hours.
6) Towards the end of the cooking time, preheat the broiler of oven. Grease a baking sheet.
7) After cooking time is finished, uncover the slow cooker and transfer the drumsticks onto the prepared baking sheet.
8) Brush the drumsticks with remaining BBQ sauce sauce evenly.

9) Broil for about 3-5 minutes.
10) Serve hot.

Glazed Chicken Legs

Cook time: 6 hours 40 minutes │Serves: 4 │ Per Serving: Calories 529, Carbs 27.9g, Fat 30g, Protein 40.3g

Ingredients:

- Garlic – 2 tsp. minced
- Ketchup – 1 C.
- Apple cider vinegar – ¼ C.
- Olive oil – 1 tbsp.
- Brown sugar – ¼ C.
- Paprika – 1½ tbsp.
- Red chili powder – 1 tbsp.
- Cayenne pepper – ½ tsp.
- Salt and ground black pepper, as required
- Water – ½ C.
- Onion – ½ C. sliced
- Chicken leg quarters – 4

Directions:

1) In a large-sized bowl, add all ingredients except for chicken legs, onion and water and mix well blended.
2) At the bottom of a slow cooker, place the water,
3) Arrange the chicken leg quarters in the pot in a single layer and top with onion slices, followed by ketchup mixture evenly.
4) Close the lid of the slow cooker and set on "Low" setting for 6 hours.
5) After cooking time is finished, uncover the slow cooker and serve hot.

Sweet Pulled Chicken

Cook time: 4 hours │Serves: 4 │ Per Serving: Calories 404, Carbs 20.6g, Fat 12.7g, Protein 50g

Ingredients:

- Low-sodium soy sauce – 3 tbsp.
- Blackberry jam – 3 tbsp.
- Maple syrup – 3 tbsp.
- Red pepper flakes – ½ tsp. crushed
- Boneless, skinless chicken breasts – 3 (8-oz.)

Directions:

1) Grease the pot of a slow cooker generously.
2) In a bowl, add all the ingredients except for the chicken breasts and mix well.
3) In the prepared pot, place the chicken breasts and top with the jam mixture.
4) Close the lid of slow cooker and set on "High" setting for 4 hours.
5) After cooking time is finished, uncover the slow cooker and with 2 forks, shred the meat.
6) Stir the shredded meat with pot sauce and serve hot.

Creamy Pulled Chicken

Cook time: 5 hours 5 minutes | Serves: 4 | Per Serving: Calories 230, Carbs 3.8g, Fat 11.7g, Protein 26.1g

Ingredients:

- Olive oil – 1 tbsp.
- Skinless, boneless chicken thighs – 4 (4-oz.)
- Salt and ground black pepper, as required
- Garlic cloves – 2, minced
- Unsweetened coconut milk – ½ C.
- Medium onion – 1, slice thinly

Directions:

1) In a large-sized wok, heat oil over a medium-high heat and cook the chicken thighs with salt and black pepper for about 4-5 minutes or until browned from all sides.
2) Transfer chicken thighs into a large-sized bowl with remaining ingredients except for onion and mix well.
3) In the pot of a slow cooker, place the sliced onion.
4) Place chicken mixture over the onion slices.
5) Close the lid of the slow cooker and set on "Low" setting for 4-5 hours.
6) After cooking time is finished, uncover the slow cooker and with 2 forks, shred the meat.
7) Stir the shredded meat with pot sauce and serve hot.

Teriyaki Chicken

Cook time: 8 hours 10 minutes │Serves: 4 │ Per Serving: Calories 310, Carbs 17.5g, Fat 10.7g, Protein 34.4g

Ingredients:

- Boneless, skinless chicken breasts – 1 lb.
- Fresh ginger – 1½ tsp. minced
- Garlic – 1½ tsp. minced
- Low-sodium soy sauce – 1/3 C.
- Rice vinegar – 2 tbsp.
- Sesame oil – 2 tsp. toasted
- Honey – 2 tbsp.
- Brown sugar – 2 tbsp.
- Cornstarch – 1 tbsp.
- Cold water – 2 tbsp.
- Sesame seeds – 1 tbsp.
- Scallion greens – 2 tbsp. sliced

Directions:

1) In a small-sized bowl, add ginger, garlic, soy sauce, vinegar, sesame oil, honey and brown sugar and beat well blended.
2) In the pot of a slow cooker, place the chicken breasts in a single layer and top with sauce mixture.
3) Close the lid of the slow cooker and set on "Low" setting for 8 hours.
4) After cooking time is finished, uncover the slow cooker and with tongs, transfer the chicken mixture into a large serving bowl.
5) .
6) Through a strainer, strain the pot sauce into a saucepan.
7) Meanwhile, in a small bowl, mix the cornstarch with water.
8) Pour the cornstarch mixture into the pan with sauce and bring a boil, stirring continuously.
9) Cook for about 1-2 minutes, stirring continuously.
10) Pour the sauce over the chicken pieces and toss to coat well.
11) Sprinkle with sesame seeds and scallion greens and serve.

Bacon-Wrapped Chicken Breast

Cook time: 8 hours | Serves: 4 | Per Serving: Calories 536, Carbs 2.1g, Fat 40.1g, Protein 60.9g

Ingredients:

- Low-fat cream cheese – ¾ C. softened
- Fresh chives – 2 tbsp. chopped
- Boneless, skinless chicken breasts – 4 (6-oz.), pounded into ½-inch thickness
- Ground black pepper, as required
- Bacon strips – 8

Directions:

1) Grease the pot of a slow cooker lightly.
2) In a bowl, add the cream cheese, chives and black pepper and mix well until blended.
3) Season the chicken breasts with a pinch of black pepper.
4) Place the cream cheese mixture in the centre of each chicken breast.
5) Wrap each chicken piece with 2 bacon strips.
6) In the prepared slow cooker, place the chicken breasts.
7) Close the lid of the slow cooker and set on "Low" setting for 6-8 hours.
8) After cooking time is finished, uncover the slow cooker and
9) Serve hot.

Stuffed Chicken Breasts

Cook time: 8 hours 5 minutes | Serves: 4 | Per Serving: Calories 233, Carbs 5.1g, Fat 8.7g, Protein 33g

Ingredients:

- Skinless, boneless chicken breasts – 4 (5-oz.)
- Olive oil – 1 tbsp.
- Small onion – 1, chopped
- Bell pepper – 1, seeded and chopped
- Garlic cloves – 2, minced
- Fresh spinach – 1 C. trimmed and chopped
- Dried oregano – ½ tsp.
- Salt and ground black pepper, as required
- Fresh lemon juice – 2 tsp.
- Low-sodium chicken broth – 1 C.

Directions:

1) With a sharp knife, make a deep cut in the middle of one side of each chicken breast to form a pocket.
2) In a non-stick saucepan, heat oil over medium heat and sauté onion and bell pepper for about 1 minute.
3) Add garlic and spinach and cook for about 2-3 minutes.
4) Stir in oregano and black pepper and remove from heat.
5) Place spinach mixture in each chicken pocket evenly.
6) Arrange chicken breasts in the pot of a slow cooker.
7) Pour lemon juice and broth over breasts.
8) Close the lid of slow cooker and set on "Low" setting for 6-8 hours.
9) After cooking time is finished, uncover the slow cooker and serve hot.

Chicken Cacciatore
Cook time: 8 hours | Serves: 4 | Per Serving: Calories 427, Carbs 20.6g, Fat 13g, Protein 55.8g

Ingredients:

- Skin-on, bone-in chicken thighs – 4 (6-oz.)
- Salt and ground black pepper, as required
- Small bell peppers – 2, seeded and chopped
- Fresh mushrooms – 6 oz. sliced
- Garlic cloves – 2, minced
- Crushed tomatoes – 1 (24-oz.) can
- Low-sodium chicken broth – ½ C.
- Dried oregano – 1 tsp.
- Red pepper flakes – ¼ tsp.
- Capers – ¼ C.

Directions:

1) Rub each chicken thigh with salt and black pepper evenly.
2) In the pot of a slow cooker, place all ingredients except for capers and stir to combine.
3) Close the lid of the slow cooker and set on "Low" setting for 6-8 hours.
4) After cooking time is finished, uncover the slow cooker and stir in the capers.
5) Serve hot.

Chicken Milano

Cook time: 5 hours | Serves: 4 | Per Serving: Calories 389, Carbs 8.5g, Fat 18.7g, Protein 48g

Ingredients:

- Chicken tenderloins – 1½ lb.
- Salt and ground black pepper, as required
- Cream of chicken soup with herbs – 5 oz.
- Cream of mushroom soup – 6 oz.
- Low-sodium chicken broth – ¼ C.
- Fresh Cremini mushrooms – 8 oz. sliced
- Fresh basil – 1½ tbsp. chopped
- Low-fat cream cheese – 4 oz. softened
- Ham slices – 1/3 lb.
- Mozzarella cheese – 1 C. shredded
- Fresh parsley – 2 tbsp. chopped

Directions:

1) Sprinkle the chicken tenderloins with salt and black pepper generously.
2) In a bowl, add the cream cheese, cream soups and broth and with an electric mixer, mix for about 2-4 minutes.
3) In the pot of a slow cooker, place the chicken tenderloins, followed by the mushrooms and basil.
4) Top with soup mixture evenly.
5) Arrange the ham slices on top and sprinkle with the mozzarella cheese.
6) Close the lid of slow cooker and set on "Low" setting for 4-5 hours.
7) After cooking time is finished, uncover the slow cooker and serve with the garnishing of parsley.

Creamy Tomato Chicken

Cook time: 6 hours | Serves: 4 | Per Serving: Calories 472, Carbs 6.5g, Fat 25.3g, Protein 52.7g

Ingredients:

- Low-sodium chicken broth – ¾ C.
- Sour cream – 1 C.
- Fresh tomatoes – 1½ C. finely chopped
- Jalapeño pepper – 1, chopped finel
- Fresh rosemary – 2 tbsp. chopped
- Salt and ground black pepper, as required
- Boneless, skinless chicken breasts – 6 (4-oz.)

Directions:

1) In the pot of a slow cooker, add all ingredients and stir to combine.

2) Close the lid of slow cooker and set on "Low" setting for 6 hours.
3) After cooking time is finished, uncover the slow cooker and serve hot.

Braised Chicken with Bacon

Cook time: 6 hours 20 minutes | Serves: 4 | Per Serving: Calories 4198, Carbs 10.3g, Fat 17g, Protein 54.7g

Ingredients:

- Bacon slices – 2
- Large yellow onion – 1, sliced thinly
- Garlic cloves – 3, minced
- Dried oregano – 1 tsp. crushed
- Dried thyme – 1 tsp. crushed
- Paprika – ½ tsp.
- Salt and ground black pepper, as required
- Whole peeled tomatoes with liquid – 1 (19-oz.) can, chopped
- Low-sodium chicken broth – ¾ C.
- Skinless, bone-in chicken thighs – 4 (6-oz.)

Directions:

1) Heat a non-stick wok over medium-high heat and cook the bacon for about 8-10 minutes, stirring frequently.
2) With a slotted spoon, transfer the bacon into a bowl.
3) Drain most of the fats from the wok.
4) In the same wok, add the onion with bacon fat and cook for about 5-6 minutes.
5) Add the garlic, dried herbs and spices and cook for about 1 minute.
6) Add the tomatoes with liquid and cook for about 2-3 minutes.
7) Transfer the tomato mixture into a slow cooker.
8) Add the chicken thighs, bacon and broth and stir to combine.
9) Close the lid of the slow cooker and set on "Low" setting for 6 hours.
10) After cooking time is finished, uncover the slow cooker and serve hot.

Butter Chicken

Cook time: 7 hours | Serves: 4 | Per Serving: Calories 376, Carbs 14.6g, Fat 15.1g, Protein 45.1g

Ingredients:

- Boneless, skinless chicken breasts – 1½ lb. cut into 1-inch pieces
- Plain Greek yogurt – 1 C.
- Onion – 1, chopped
- Fresh ginger – 1 tbsp. grated
- Garlic cloves – 2, minced
- Jalapeño peppers – 2, minced
- Garam masala powder – 1 tsp.
- Ground cumin – 1 tsp.
- Ground coriander – 1 tsp.
- Ground turmeric – 1 tsp.
- Salt and ground black pepper, as required
- Diced tomatoes – 1 (18-oz.) can
- Unsalted butter – 3 tbsp. chopped
- Heavy cream – ¼ C.
- Fresh cilantro – 2 tbsp. chopped

Directions:

1) In the pot of a slow cooker, add chicken pieces, yogurt, onion, ginger, garlic, jalapeño peppers, spices, salt and black pepper and mix well.
2) Place the tomatoes over the chicken mixture and gently stir to combine.
3) Place the butter pieces on top evenly.
4) Close the lid of slow cooker and set on "Low" setting for 6-7 hours.
5) After cooking time is finished, uncover the slow cooker and stir in the heavy cream.
6) Serve hot with the garnishing of cilantro.

Chicken & Veggie Curry

Cook time: 6 hours | Serves: 4 | Per Serving: Calories 374, Carbs 13.5g, Fat 21g, Protein 29.7g

Ingredients:

- Unsweetened coconut milk – 1½ C.
- Red curry paste – 2 tbsp.
- Skinless, boneless chicken breasts – 1 lb. cubed
- Small white onion – 1, chopped
- Garlic cloves – 2, chopped
- Head cauliflower – ½, chopped
- Fresh green peas – 1 C. shelled

Directions:

1) In a bowl, blend together coconut milk and curry paste.
2) In the pot of a slow cooker, place curry mixture.
3) Add remaining ingredients and mix well.
4) Close the lid of slow cooker and set on "Low" setting for 6 hours.
5) After cooking time is finished, uncover the slow cooker and serve hot.

Chicken in Wine Sauce

Cook time: 6 hours │Serves: 4 │ Per Serving: Calories 486, Carbs 9.1g, Fat 19.8g, Protein 50.5g

Ingredients:

- Boneless, skinless chicken breasts – 1½ lb. cut into 1-inch chunks
- Medium tomatoes – 2, grated
- Onion – 1, finely chopped
- Garlic clove – 1, minced
- White wine – 1½ C.
- Extra-virgin olive oil – 2 tbsp.
- Tomato paste – 2 tbsp.
- Allspice berries – 2
- Cinnamon stick – 1
- Whole cloves – 2
- Salt and ground black pepper, as required

Directions:

1) In the pot of a slow cooker, place all ingredients and stir to combine.
2) Close the lid of the slow cooker and set on "High" setting for 6 hours.
3) After cooking time is finished, uncover the slow cooker and serve hot.

Chicken with Olives

Cook time: 5¼ hours | Serves: 4 | Per Serving: Calories 364, Carbs 8.9g, Fat 17.1g, Protein 42.8g

Ingredients:

- Olive oil – 1 tbsp.
- Boneless, skinless chicken thighs – 4 (5-oz.)
- Onion – 1, sliced thinly
- Garlic cloves – 2, minced
- Roasted red peppers – 1 C. chopped
- Olives – ¾ C. pitted
- Low-sodium chicken broth – ½ C.
- Capers – 1 tbsp.
- Bay leaf – 1
- Dried rosemary – 1 tsp.
- Dried thyme – 1 tsp.
- Dried oregano – 1 tsp.
- Salt and ground black pepper, as required
- Fresh lemon juice – 2 tbsp.

Directions:

1) In a non-stick wok, heat oil over medium-high heat and cook the chicken thighs for about 4-5 minutes per side or until browned
2) With a slotted spoon, transfer the chicken thighs onto a plate.
3) In the same wok, add the onion and garlic and sauté for about 4-5 minutes.
4) In the pot of a slow cooker, add the cooked chicken thighs, onion mixture and remaining ingredients except for lemon juice and stir to combine.
5) Close the lid of the slow cooker and set on "Low" setting for 4-5 hours.
6) After cooking time is finished, uncover the slow cooker and stir in the lemon juice. Remove the bay leaf.
7) Serve hot.

Chicken with Broccoli & Mushrooms

Cook time: 6 hours | Serves: 4 | Per Serving: Calories 171, Carbs 5.1g, Fat 4.2g, Protein 27.8g

Ingredients:

- Skinless, boneless chicken thighs – 1 lb. cubed
- Low-sodium chicken broth – 1½ C.
- Small white onion – 1, chopped
- Garlic cloves – 2, minced
- Broccoli – 1¼ C. chopped
- Fresh mushrooms – 1¼ C. sliced
- Salt and ground black pepper, as required

Directions:

1) In the pot of a slow cooker, add all ingredients and mix well.
2) Close the lid of slow cooker and set on "Low" setting for 5-6 hours.
3) After cooking time is finished, uncover the slow cooker and serve hot.

Chicken with Potatoes

Cook time: 8 hours 6 minutes | Serves: 4 | Per Serving: Calories 522, Carbs 18.6g, Fat 24.4g, Protein 55.4g

Ingredients:

- Dried oregano – ½ tsp.
- Dried basil – ½ tsp.
- Dried rosemary – ¼ tsp.
- Salt and ground black pepper, as required
- Bone-in, skin-on chicken thighs – 4 (6-oz.)
- Unsalted butter – 2 tbsp.
- Baby red potatoes – 1 lb. quartered
- Olive oil – 1 tbsp.
- Garlic cloves – 2, minced
- Parmesan cheese – ½ C. grated
- Fresh parsley – 2 tbsp. chopped

Directions:

1) In a bowl, add the oregano, basil, rosemary, salt and black pepper and mix well.
2) Season the chicken thighs with herb mixture generously.
3) In a large-sized non-stick wok, melt butter over a medium-high heat.
4) Place the chicken thighs, skin-side down and cook for about 2-3 minutes.
5) Flip and cook for about 2-3 minutes.
6) In the pot of a slow cooker, place the potatoes, oil and garlic, salt and black pepper and stir to combine.
7) Arrange the chicken thighs on top in an even layer.
8) Close the lid of the slow cooker and set on "Low" setting for 7-8 hours.
9) After cooking time is finished, uncover the slow cooker and sprinkle the top with Parmesan and parsley.
10) Serve immediately.

Chicken with Pumpkin

Cook time: 3 hours | Serves: 4 | Per Serving: Calories 248, Carbs 7.3g, Fat 8.7g, Protein 34.2g

Ingredients:

- Boneless, skinless chicken breasts – 1 lb. chopped
- Pumpkin – 8 oz. peeled and chopped
- Small yellow onion – 1, chopped
- Ground cumin – 1 tsp.
- Ground cinnamon – 1 tsp.
- Ground allspice – ¼ tsp.
- Salt and ground black pepper, as required
- Low-sodium chicken broth – 1 C.

Directions:

1) Grease the pot of a slow cooker generously.
2) In the prepared pot, place all the ingredients and stir to combine.
3) Close the lid of the slow cooker and set on "High" setting for 3 hours.
4) After cooking time is finished, uncover the slow cooker and serve hot.

Chicken with Artichokes

Cook time: 7 hours 21 minutes | Serves: 4 | Per Serving: Calories 184, Carbs 9.3g, Fat 4.2g, Protein 27.4g

Ingredients:

- Olive oil – 2 tbsp.
- Skinless, boneless chicken breast halves – 4 (4-oz.)
- Frozen artichoke hearts – 6 oz.
- Onion – 1/3 C. chopped
- Garlic cloves – 4, minced
- Low-sodium chicken broth – ½ C.
- Dried rosemary – 1 tsp. crushed
- Salt and ground black pepper, as required
- Cornstarch – 1 tbsp.
- Cold water – 1 tbsp.

Directions:

1) In a large-sized non-stick wok, heat oil over medium heat and cook the chicken breast halves for about 2-3 minutes per side or until browned.
2) In the pot of a slow cooker, blend together the artichoke hearts, onion, garlic, broth, rosemary, salt and black pepper.
3) Arrange the browned chicken on top in a single layer.
4) Place some of the garlic mixture over chicken.

5) Close the lid of the slow cooker and set on "Low" setting for 6-7 hours.
6) After cooking time is finished, uncover the slow cooker and with a slotted spoon, transfer the chicken and artichokes onto a platter.
7) With a piece of foil, cover the chicken and artichokes to keep warm.
8) In a small-sized bowl, dissolve the cornstarch into water.
9) Add the cornstarch mixture into the slow cooker, stirring continuously.
10) Close the lid of the slow cooker and set on "High" setting for 15 minutes.
11) After cooking time is finished, uncover the slow cooker and place the sauce over chicken and artichokes.
12) Serve hot.

Chicken with Spinach

Cook time: 5 hours │Serves: 4 │ Per Serving: Calories 236, Carbs 3.7g, Fat 8.5g, Protein 34.3g

Ingredients:

- Boneless chicken breasts – 1 lb. Cut into bite-sized pieces
- Fresh spinach – 4-5 C. chopped
- Onion – 1, sliced thinly
- Garlic cloves – 1, minced
- Low-sodium chicken broth – 1 C.
- Cayenne pepper – ¼ tsp.
- Salt and ground black pepper, as required

Directions:

1) In the pot of a slow cooker, add all ingredients and mix well.
2) Close the lid of the slow cooker and set on "Low" setting for 5 hours.
3) After cooking time is finished, uncover the slow cooker and serve hot.

Chicken with Zoodles & Asparagus

Cook time: 8½ hours │Serves: 4 │ Per Serving: Calories 294, Carbs 8.6g, Fat 15.1g, Protein 32g

Ingredients:

- Skinless, boneless chicken breast tenders – 1 lb.
- Small onion – 1, chopped
- Asparagus – 1 C. trimmed and cut into 2-inch pieces
- Fresh thyme – 1 tbsp. chopped
- Garlic powder – 1 tsp.
- Salt and ground black pepper, as required

- Medium zucchinis – 2, spiralized with blade C
- Light sour cream – ½ C.
- Cheddar cheese – ½ C. shredded

Directions:

1) In the pot of a slow cooker, add chicken, onion, asparagus, thyme, garlic powder and black pepper and mix.
2) Close the lid of the slow cooker and set on "Low" setting for 6-8 hours.
3) After cooking time is finished, uncover the slow cooker and place zucchini noodles over the chicken.
4) Top with cheese and cream.
5) Close the lid of the slow cooker and set on "High" setting for 30 minutes.
6) After cooking time is finished, uncover the slow cooker and gently stir the chicken mixture.
7) Serve hot.

Chicken with Quinoa

Cook time: 8 hours 5 minutes │Serves: 4 │ Per Serving: Calories 299, Carbs 31.9g, Fat 8.3g, Protein 25.7g

Ingredients:

- Olive oil – 1 tbsp.
- Small onion – 1, chopped
- Fresh ginger – 1 tsp. minced
- Garlic cloves – 2, minced
- Skinless, boneless chicken breasts – 3 (5-oz.)
- Butternut squash – 1½ C. peeled and cubed
- Tomatoes – 1 C. chopped
- Quinoa – ½ C. rinsed
- Dried oregano – 1 tsp. crushed
- Curry powder – 2 tsp.
- Cayenne pepper – ½ tsp.
- Salt and ground black pepper, as required
- Low-sodium vegetable broth – 3½ C.

Directions:

1) In a non-stick wok, heat oil over medium heat and sauté onion and garlic for about 4-5 minutes.
2) Transfer the onion mixture into a slow cooker.
3) Add remaining ingredients and stir to combine.
4) Close the lid of the slow cooker and set on "Low" setting for 7-8 hours.
5) After cooking time is finished, uncover the slow cooker and transfer the chicken breasts into a bowl.
6) With 2 forks, shred the meat of the chicken breasts completely.
7) Add the shredded chicken into the quinoa mixture and stir to combine.
8) Serve hot.

Chicken with Beans

Cook time: 8¼ hours | Serves: 4 | Per Serving: Calories 348, Carbs 39.2g, Fat 4.2g, Protein 37.9g

Ingredients:

- Olive oil – 1 tbsp.
- Onion – 1, chopped
- Garlic cloves – 2, minced
- Skinless, boneless chicken breasts – 1 lb.
- Ground cumin – 1 tsp.
- Tomatoes – 1½ C. chopped
- Black beans – 1 (15-oz.) can, rinsed and drained
- White beans – ½ (15-oz.) can, rinsed and drained
- Cayenne pepper – ½ tsp.
- Salt and ground black pepper, as required
- Low-sodium chicken broth – 1 C.

Directions:

1) In a large-sized non-stick wok, heat oil over medium heat and cook onions for about 5-6 minutes.
2) Add garlic and cook for about 1 minute.
3) Add chicken and cook for about 3-4 minutes per side or until browned.
4) Transfer the chicken mixture into the pot of a slow cooker.
5) Add remaining ingredients and stir to combine.
6) Close the lid of the slow cooker and set on "Low" setting for 8 hours.
7) After cooking time is finished, uncover the slow cooker and transfer the chicken into a bowl.
8) With 2 forks, shred the meat of chicken breasts completely.
9) Add the shredded chicken into the beans mixture and stir to combine.
10) Serve hot.

Chicken with Chickpeas & Sweet Potato

Cook time: 5 hours | Serves: 4 | Per Serving: Calories 292, Carbs 31.2g, Fat 4.7g, Protein 31.2g

Ingredients:

- Boneless, skinless chicken breasts – 1 lb.
- Large sweet potato – 1, peeled and chopped
- Small onion – 1, chopped
- Garlic cloves – 2, minced
- Large carrot – 2, peeled and chopped
- Canned chickpeas – 8 oz. rinsed and drained

- Diced tomatoes with juices – 1 (14-oz.) can
- Dried parsley – 1 tsp.
- Ground turmeric – ½ tsp.
- Ground cumin ½ tsp.
- Ground cinnamon – ¼ tsp.
- Salt and ground black pepper, as required

Directions:

1) In the pot of a slow cooker, place all ingredients and stir to combine.
2) Close the lid of the slow cooker and set on "High" setting for 4-5 hours.
3) After cooking time is finished, uncover the slow cooker and serve hot.

Chicken with Orzo & Mushrooms

Cook time: 3 hours 5 minutes │Serves: 4 │ Per Serving: Calories 5108, Carbs 20.6g, Fat 27.5g, Protein 41.7g

Ingredients:

- Boneless, skinless chicken breasts – 4 (4-oz.)
- Italian seasoning – 3 tsp. divided
- Salt and ground black pepper, as required
- Olive oil – 3 tsp.
- Fresh mushrooms – 1 C. slice
- Medium onion – 1, finely chopped
- Garlic – 2 tsp. minced
- Unsalted butter – 4 tbsp. melted
- Low-sodium chicken broth – 3 C.
- Orzo pasta – 1 C.
- Parmesan cheese – ½ C. shredded

Directions:

1) Grease the pot of a slow cooker.
2) Season the chicken breasts with a little Italian seasoning, salt and black pepper evenly.
3) In a large-sized non-stick wok, heat the oil over medium-high heat and cook the chicken breasts for about 5 minutes, flipping once halfway through.
4) Transfer the chicken breasts into the prepared slow cooker.
5) Top with mushrooms, onions, garlic, butter, broth, remaining Italian seasoning, salt and black pepper.
6) Close the lid of the slow cooker and set on "High" setting for 2 hours.
7) After cooking time is finished, uncover the slow cooker and stir in the orzo.
8) Again, close the lid of slow cooker and set on "High" setting for 30-45 minutes.
9) After cooking time is finished, uncover the slow cooker and with a slotted spoon transfer the chicken breasts into a bowl.

10) With 2 forks, shred the chicken meat.
11) Return the shredded chicken into the slow cooker and stir to combine.
12) Sprinkle the top with the Parmesan cheese evenly.
13) Close the lid of the slow cooker and set on "High" setting for 15 minutes.
14) After cooking time is finished, uncover the slow cooker and serve hot.

Chicken & Peas Risotto

Cook time: 3 hours 25 minutes | Serves: 4 | Per Serving: Calories 529, Carbs 61.6g, Fat 11g, Protein 42.4g

Ingredients:

- Olive oil – 1½ tbsp.
- Onion – 1, finely chopped
- Garlic – 1 tsp. crushed
- Arborio rice – 1¼ C.
- Boneless, skinless chicken breasts, 1 lb. chopped in small pieces
- Low-sodium chicken broth – 3 C.
- Water – ¾ C.
- Dry white wine – ¼ C.
- Dried chilli flakes – ½ tsp.
- Frozen peas 2 C.
- Parmesan cheese ¾ C. grated freshly

Directions:

1) In a heavy-bottomed saucepan, heat 1 tbsp. of oil over a medium-high heat and cook the onion and garlic for about 2 minutes.
2) Add rice and cook for about 2 minutes, stirring continuously.
3) Transfer the rice mixture into the pot of a slow cooker.
4) In the same saucepan, add chicken pieces over a medium-high heat and cook for about 5-6 minutes.
5) Transfer the chicken pieces into the pot of slow cooker.
6) In the pot, add broth, water, wine and chilli flakes and stir to combine.
7) Close the lid of the slow cooker and set on "High" setting for 2½-3 hours.
8) After cooking time is finished, uncover the slow cooker and stir in the peas.
9) Again, close the lid of the slow cooker and set on "High" setting for 15 minutes.
10) After cooking time is finished, uncover the slow cooker and stir in the Parmesan.
11) Serve hot.

Ground Chicken with Pea

Cook time: 8¼ hours | Serves: 4 | Per Serving: Calories 288, Carbs 11.6g, Fat 10.8g, Protein 35.7g

Ingredients:

- Unsalted butter – 2 tsp.
- Medium onion – 1, finely chopped
- Jalapeño peppers – 2, seeded and chopped
- Fresh ginger – 1 tsp. grated
- Garlic cloves – 3, minced
- Ground chicken – 1 lb.
- Salt, as required
- Tomato sauce – ¾ C.
- Water – ¼ C.
- Red chili powder – 1 tsp.
- Ground coriander – ¾ tsp.
- Ground cumin – ¾ tsp.
- Ground turmeric – ¾ tsp.
- Garam masala powder – ¾ tsp.
- Bay leaf – 1
- Frozen peas – ¾ C.
- Fresh cilantro – 2 tbsp. chopped

Directions:

1) In a large-sized non-stick wok, melt butter over medium heat and cook the onion for about 6-8 minutes.
2) Add the jalapeño peppers, ginger and garlic and cook for about 1 minute.
3) Add the ground chicken and salt and cook for about 5-6 minutes.
4) Transfer the chicken mixture into a slow cooker.
5) Add the remaining ingredients except for peas and cilantro and stir to combine.
6) Close the lid of the slow cooker and set on "Low" setting for 6-7½ hours.
7) After cooking time is finished, uncover the slow cooker and stir in the peas.
8) Close the lid of the slow cooker and set on "High" setting for 30 minutes.
9) After cooking time is finished, uncover the slow cooker and discard the bay leaf.
10) Serve hot with the garnishing of cilantro.

Beef Recipes

Lemony Beef Chuck

Cook time: 10 hours | Serves: 4 | Per Serving: Calories 422, Carbs 4.6g, Fat 23.5g, Protein 46.3g

Ingredients:

- Beef chuck roast – 1½ lb. trimmed
- Large onion – 1, sliced thinly
- Extra-virgin olive – oil ¼ C.
- Garlic – 1 tbsp. minced
- Dried oregano – 1 tsp.
- Salt and ground black pepper, as required
- Fresh lemon juice – 3 tbsp.

Directions:

1) In the pot of a slow cooker, place all ingredients and stir to combine.
2) Close the lid of the slow cooker and set on "Low" setting for 8-10 hours.
3) After cooking time is finished, uncover the slow cooker and place the roast onto a cutting board for about 12-15 minutes before slicing
4) Cut into desired-sized slices and serve.

Braised Beef Pot Roast

Cook time: 8 hours | Serves: 4 | Per Serving: Calories 362, Carbs 4.3g, Fat 8.9g, Protein 62.3g

Ingredients:

- Beef pot roast – 1½ lb. trimmed
- Onion – 1, sliced
- Garlic cloves – 2, minced
- Fresh rosemary – 1 tbsp. minced
- Ground cumin – 1 tsp.
- Paprika – 1 tsp.
- Salt and ground black pepper, as required
- Fresh lemon juice – 2-3 tbsp.
- Low-sodium beef broth – ½ C.

Directions:

1) In the pot of a slow cooker, add all ingredients and mix well.
2) Close the lid of the slow cooker and set on "Low" setting for 8 hours.
3) After cooking time is finished, uncover the slow cooker and place the roast onto a cutting board for about 13-15 minutes before slicing.

4) Cut into desired-sized slices and serve.

Braised Beef Shanks

Cook time: 6 hours | Serves: 4 | Per Serving: Calories 491, Carbs 2.8g, Fat 16.5g, Protein 77.7g

Ingredients:

- Beef shanks – 2 lb.
- Garlic cloves – 3, minced
- Italian seasoning – 2 tbsp.
- Dried oregano – 1 tsp.
- Onion powder – ½ tsp.
- Salt and ground black pepper, as required
- Low-sodium beef broth – 2 C.

Directions:

1) In the pot of a slow cooker, place all ingredients and mix well.
2) Close the lid of the slow cooker and set on "High" setting for 4-6 hours.
3) After cooking time is finished, uncover the slow cooker and serve hot.

Spiced Braised Beef Ribs

Cook time: 8 hours 5 minutes | Serves: 4 | Per Serving: Calories 471, Carbs 5g, Fat 15.2g, Protein 72.7g

Ingredients:

- Beef short ribs – 2 lb.
- Salt and ground black pepper, as required
- Low-sodium beef broth – 2 C.
- Worcestershire sauce – ¼ C.
- Onion powder – 1 tsp.
- Garlic powder – 1 tsp.
- Fresh rosemary sprig – 1

Directions:

1) Season the short ribs with salt and black pepper evenly.
2) Heat a large-sized non-stick wok over high heat and sear the ribs for about 3-5 minutes or until browned from all sides.
3) In the pot of a slow cooker, add broth, Worcestershire sauce, onion powder and garlic powder mix well.
4) Place the ribs in the broth mixture.
5) Arrange rosemary sprig on top of ribs.
6) Close the lid of the slow cooker and set on "Low" setting for 6-8 hours.

7) After cooking time is finished, uncover the slow cooker and serve hot.

Tomato Braised Beef Ribs

Cook time: 8 hours | Serves: 4 | Per Serving: Calories 517, Carbs 10.6g, Fat 20.8g, Protein 68.4g

Ingredients:

- Low-sodium beef broth – 1 C.
- Garlic cloves – 2, minced
- Smoked paprika – 1 tsp.
- Salt and ground black pepper, as required
- Beef short ribs – 2 lb.
- Tomato paste – 1 C.
- Green chilies – 2 tbsp. chopped

Directions:

1) In a bowl, blend together broth, garlic, paprika, salt and black pepper and keep aside.
2) In the pot of a slow cooker, place beef ribs and top with tomato paste and green chilies.
3) Pour broth mixture on top.
4) Close the lid of the slow cooker and set on "Low" setting for 6-8 hours.
5) After cooking time is finished, uncover the slow cooker and serve hot.

Wine Braised Beef Brisket

Cook time: 8 hours | Serves: 4 | Per Serving: Calories 417, Carbs 8.4g, Fat 13.3g, Protein 53g

Ingredients:

- Beef brisket – 1½ lb. trimmed
- Salt and ground black pepper, as required
- Olive oil – 2 tsp.
- Medium onion – 1, chopped
- Garlic cloves – 2, sliced
- Herbes de Provence – 1 tbsp.
- Diced tomatoes – 1 (15-oz.) can, drained
- Dijon mustard – 2 tsp.
- Dry red wine – 1 C.

Directions:

1) Season the brisket with salt and black pepper evenly.
2) In a non-stick wok, heat oil over medium heat and cook the brisket for about 4-5 minutes per side.
3) Transfer the brisket into a slow cooker.

4) Add the remaining ingredients and stir to combine.
5) Close the lid of the slow cooker and set on "Low" setting for 8 hours.
6) After cooking time is finished, uncover the slow cooker and with a slotted spoon, transfer the brisket onto a platter.
7) Cut the brisket into desired sized slices and serve with the topping of pan sauce.

Garlicky Pulled Beef

Cook time: 10 hours │Serves: 4 │ Per Serving: Calories 468, Carbs 3.7g, Fat 28.6g, Protein 46g

Ingredients:

- Boneless beef – 1½ lb. trimmed
- Whole garlic cloves – 4, peeled
- Onion – 1, sliced
- Salt and ground black pepper, as required
- Low-sodium beef broth – ½ C.

Directions:

1) With a sharp knife, make 4 deep cuts in different places of beef.
2) Press the garlic cloves into each cut.
3) In the pot of a slow cooker, place onion slices.
4) Place beef over onion slices and sprinkle with salt and black pepper.
5) Pour the broth on top.
6) Close the lid of the slow cooker and set on "Low" setting for 8-10 hours.
7) After cooking time is finished, uncover the slow cooker and with 2 forks, shred the meat.
8) Stir the shredded meat with pot sauce and serve hot.

Creamy Pulled Beef

Cook time: 7¼ hours │Serves: 4 │ Per Serving: Calories 364, Carbs 2.5g, Fat 14.8g, Protein 52g

Ingredients:

- Beef pot roast – 1½-lb. trimmed
- Italian salad dressing – ¼ C.
- Low-sodium chicken broth – ½ C.
- Small onion – ½, chopped
- Dry Italian dressing – ½ packet

Directions:

1) In the pot of a slow cooker, place all the ingredients, except for the dressing packet and stir to combine.
2) Close the lid of the slow cooker and set on "High" setting for 4 hours.
3) Now set the slow cooker on "Low" setting for 3 hours.
4) After cooking time is finished, uncover the slow cooker and with 2 forks, shred the meat.
5) Add the dressing packet and stir to combine.
6) Close the lid of the slow cooker and set on "High" setting for 10-15 minutes.
7) After cooking time is finished, uncover the slow cooker and stir the mixture well.
8) Serve hot.

Mongolian Beef

Cook time: 3 hours │Serves: 4 │ Per Serving: Calories 392, Carbs 2.3g, Fat 17.7g, Protein 54.1g

Ingredients:

- Flank steak – 1½ lb. trimmed and cut into thin slices
- Unflavored gelatin powder – 2 tbsp.
- Low-sodium soy sauce – ¼ C.
- Olive oil – 1 tbsp.
- Garlic cloves – 2, minced
- Brown sugar – 2 tbsp.
- Ground ginger – ½ tsp.
- Ground black pepper, as required
- Scallion greens – 3 tbsp. sliced

Directions:

1) In a large-sized bowl, add the steak slices and gelatin powder and toss to coat.
2) In another large-sized bowl, add the remaining ingredients except for scallion and stir to combine.
3) In the pot of a slow cooker, place the steak and top with oil mixture evenly.
4) Close the lid of the slow cooker and set on "High" setting for 3 hours.
5) After cooking time is finished, uncover the slow cooker and serve hot with the garnishing of scallion greens.

Beef & Tomato Curry

Cook time: 5 hours │ Serves: 4 │ Per Serving: Calories 320, Carbs 4.6g, Fat 17.8g, Protein 34.6g

Ingredients:

- Boneless beef – 1¼ lb. trimmed and cubed
- Fresh tomatoes – 1½ C. finely chopped
- Low-sodium beef broth – 1 C.
- Unsweetened coconut milk – ½ C.
- Curry powder – 1 tbsp.
- Salt and ground black pepper, as required
- Fresh parsley – 2 tbsp.

Directions:

1) In the pot of a slow cooker, place all the ingredients and stir to combine.
2) Close the lid of the slow cooker and set on "High" setting for 5 hours.
3) After cooking time is finished, uncover the slow cooker and serve hot.

Beef & Potato Curry

Cook time: 8 hours 5 minutes │ Serves: 4 │ Per Serving: Calories 322, Carbs 24.4g, Fat 8.1g, Protein 38.2g

Ingredients:

- Beef stew meat – 1 lb. trimmed and cubed
- Small potatoes – ¾ lb. scrubbed and quartered
- Diced fire-roasted tomatoes with juices – 2 (14-oz.) cans
- Fresh ginger – 1 tbsp. grated
- Garlic cloves – 2, grated
- Curry powder – 2 tbsp.
- Ground cumin – 1 ¼ tsp.
- Salt and ground black pepper, as required
- Fresh cilantro – 2-3 tbsp.

Directions:

1) In the pot of a slow cooker, place all ingredients except for cilantro and stir to combine.
2) Close the lid of the slow cooker and set on "Low" setting for 7 hours.
3) After cooking time is finished, uncover the slow cooker and serve hot with the garnishing of cilantro.

Creamy Beef & Spinach

Cook time: 6¼ hours | Serves: 4 | Per Serving: Calories 387, Carbs 5.2g, Fat 20.1g, Protein 44.7g

Ingredients:

- Boneless beef – 1¼ lb. trimmed and cubed
- Heavy cream – 1 C.
- Large onion – 1, quartered
- Salt and ground black pepper, as required
- Fresh spinach – 3 C. chopped

Directions:

1) In the pot of a slow cooker, place all ingredients except for the spinach and stir to combine.
2) Close the lid of the slow cooker and set on "High" setting for 5-6 hours.
3) After cooking time is finished, uncover the slow cooker and immediately stir in the spinach.
4) Close the lid of the slow cooker and set on "High" setting for 10-15 minutes.
5) After cooking time is finished, uncover the slow cooker and serve hot.

Fajita Beef with Bell Peppers

Cook time: 7 hours 5 minutes | Serves: 4 | Per Serving: Calories 414, Carbs 10.5g, Fat 16.6g, Protein 53g

Ingredients:

- Unsalted butter – 2 tbsp.
- Yellow onion – 1, sliced
- Boneless beef – 1¼ lb. trimmed and sliced thinly
- Fajita seasoning – 2 tbsp.
- Bell peppers – 2, seeded and sliced
- Diced tomatoes with green chiles – ½ (14-oz.) can

Directions:

1) In a non-stick wok, melt the butter over medium-high heat and cook onion for about 2 minutes.
2) Add the beef and fajita seasoning and cook for about 2-3 minutes.
3) Transfer the beef mixture into the pot of a slow cooker.
4) Add the bell peppers and tomatoes and stir to combine.
5) Close the lid of the slow cooker and set on "Low" setting for 7 hours.
6) After cooking time is finished, uncover the slow cooker and serve hot.

Beef with Broccoli

Cook time: 5½ hours | Serves: 4 | Per Serving: Calories 374, Carbs 10.4g, Fat

Ingredients:

- Low-sodium beef broth – 1 C.
- Low-sodium soy sauce – ¼ C.
- Dark brown sugar – 2 tbsp.
- Sesame oil – 1 tbsp.
- Garlic cloves – 2, minced
- Boneless beef chuck roast – 1 lb. trimmed and cut into thin strips
- Cornstarch – 2 tbsp.
- Water – 2-3 tbsp.
- Frozen broccoli florets – 2 C.

Directions:

1) In a medium-sized bowl, whisk together the broth, soy sauce, sesame oil, brown sugar and garlic.
2) In the pot of a slow cooker, place the beef strips and top with broth mixture.
3) Close the lid of the slow cooker and set on "Low" setting for 5 hours.
4) Meanwhile, in a small-sized bowl, whisk together the cornstarch and water.
5) After cooking time is finished, uncover the slow cooker and stir in the broccoli and cornstarch mixture.
6) Close the lid of the slow cooker and set on "Low" setting for 30 minutes.
7) After cooking time is finished, uncover the slow cooker and serve hot.

Beef with Green Beans

Cook time: 8 hours | Serves: 4 | Per Serving: Calories 252, Carbs 10.6g, Fat 7.3g, Protein 36.7g

Ingredients:

- Beef flank steak – 1 lb. trimmed and cut into thin strips
- Salt and ground black pepper, as required
- Medium onion – 1, sliced
- Tomatoes – 1 C. finely chopped
- Garlic clove – 1, minced
- Fresh green beans – 2¼ C. trimmed and sliced
- Low-sodium beef broth – ½ C.

Directions:

1) In the pot of a slow cooker, add all ingredients and stir to combine.
2) Close the lid of the slow cooker and set on "Low" setting for 8 hours.
3) After cooking time is finished, uncover the slow cooker and serve hot.

Beef with Asparagus

Cook time: 8¼ hours | Serves: 4 | Per Serving: Calories 271, Carbs 6.1g, Fat 10.7g, Protein 36.7g

Ingredients:

- Olive oil – 1 tbsp.
- Beef flank steak – 1 lb. trimmed and cubed
- Salt and ground black pepper, as required
- Medium onion – 1, finely chopped
- Tomatoes – ½ C. finely chopped
- Asparagus – 2 C. trimmed and sliced
- Low-sodium beef broth – ½ C.

Directions:

1) In a large-sized wok, heat oil over a medium-high heat and cook the beef with salt and black pepper for about 4-5 minutes.
2) Transfer the beef into the pot of a slow cooker.
3) In the same wok, add onion and sauté for about 6-7 minutes.
4) Add tomatoes and cook for 2-3 minutes, crushing with the back of spoon.
5) Transfer the onion mixture into the slow cooker.
6) Add remaining ingredients and mix well.
7) Close the lid of the slow cooker and set on "Low" setting for 8 hours.
8) After cooking time is finished, uncover the slow cooker and serve hot.

Beef with Artichokes

Cook time: 7 hours 5 minutes | Serves: 4 | Per Serving: Calories 330, Carbs 15.6g, Fat 12.2g, Protein 39.9g

Ingredients:

- Vegetable oil – 1 tbsp.
- Beef stew meat – 1 lb. trimmed and cubed
- Canned artichoke hearts – 8 oz.
- Small onion – 1, chopped
- Garlic cloves – 2, chopped
- Low-sodium beef broth – 1 C.
- Tomato sauce – 1 (6-oz.) can
- Diced tomatoes with juices 1 (14-oz.) can
- Kalamata olives – 1/3 C. pitted
- Dried oregano – 1 tsp.
- Dried basil – 1 tsp.
- Ground cumin – ½ tsp.
- Bay leaf – 1

Directions:

1) In a non-stick wok, heat oil over medium-high heat and cook the beef for about 5 minutes.
2) Transfer the beef into the pot of a slow cooker and top with artichoke hearts, followed by the onion and garlic.
3) Place the remaining ingredients on top.
4) Close the lid of the slow cooker and set on "Low" setting for 7 hours.
5) After cooking time is finished, uncover the slow cooker and stir the mixture.
6) Serve hot.

Beef with Mushrooms

Cook time: 9 hours | Serves: 4 | Per Serving: Calories 279, Carbs 14.2g, Fat 7.6g, Protein 39.1g

Ingredients:

- Beef stew meat – 1 lb. cut into 4 portions
- Fresh mushrooms – 1½ C. sliced
- Garlic cloves – 2, minced
- Fresh parsley leaves – ¼ C. chopped
- Tomato paste – 1 C.
- Low-sodium beef broth – 1 C.
- Salt and ground black pepper, as required
- Fresh lemon juice – 2 tbsp.

Directions:

1) In the pot of a slow cooker, add all ingredients except for lemon juice and, stir to combine.
2) Close the lid of the slow cooker and set on "Low" setting for 8-9 hours.
3) After cooking time is finished, uncover the slow cooker and serve hot with the drizzling of lemon juice

Beef with Olives

Cook time: 8 hours | Serves: 4 | Per Serving: Calories 298, Carbs 3.4g, Fat 15.3g, Protein 35.4g

Ingredients:

- Boneless beef stew meat – 1 lb. trimmed and cubed
- Black olives – 1½ C. pitted and halved
- Unsalted butter – 1 tbsp. Melted
- Salt and ground black pepper, as required
- Low-sodium chicken broth – 1 C.

Directions:

1) In the pot of a slow cooker, add all ingredients and stir to combine.
2) Close the lid of the slow cooker and set on "Low" setting for 7-8 hours.
3) After cooking time is finished, uncover the slow cooker and serve hot.

Beef with Squash & Cherries

Cook time: 8 hours 10 minutes |Serves: 4 | Per Serving: Calories 430, Carbs 42.2g, Fat 10.8g, Protein 35.9g

Ingredients:

- Coconut oil – 2 tsp.
- Boneless beef – 1 lb. trimmed and cubed
- Small onion – 1, chopped
- Fresh thyme– ½ tbsp. chopped
- Fresh sage – ½ tbsp. chopped
- Low-sodium beef broth - 1½ C.
- Ground allspice – ½ tsp.
- Ground nutmeg – ¼ tsp.
- Bay leaf – 1
- Butternut squash – 2 C. peeled and cubed
- Dried cherries – 1 C.
- Salt and ground black pepper, as required

Directions:

1) In a non-stick wok, melt coconut oil over medium heat and sear the beef for about 4-5 minutes or until browned.
2) With a slotted spoon, transfer the beef into a slow cooker.
3) In the same wok, add onion, thyme and sage and cook for 4-5 minutes.
4) Transfer the onion mixture into the slow cooker,
5) In the slow cooker, add the broth, nutmeg, all spices and bay leaf and stir to combine.
6) Close the lid of the slow cooker and set on "Low" setting for 6 hours.
7) After cooking time is finished, uncover the slow cooker and stir in the butternut squash, cherries, salt and black pepper.
8) Close the lid of the slow cooker and set on "Low" setting for 2 hours.
9) After cooking time is finished, uncover the slow cooker and serve hot.

Ground Beef with Mushrooms

Cook time: 4 hours 10 minutes | Serves: 4 | Per Serving: Calories 226, Carbs 3.2g, Fat 7.2g, Protein 35.8g

Ingredients:

- Lean ground beef – 1 lb.
- Salt and ground black pepper, as required
- Fresh mushrooms – 1½ C. sliced
- Tomato sauce – 6 oz.
- Water – 1¼ C.
- Fresh parsley – ¼ C. chopped

Directions:

1) Heat a greased wok over medium heat and cook the beef with salt and black pepper for about 4-5 minutes.
2) Add the mushrooms and cook for about 4-5 minutes.
3) Transfer the beef mixture into the pot of a slow cooker.
4) Add the tomato sauce and water and stir to combine.
5) Close the lid of the slow cooker and set on "High" setting for 4 hours.
6) After cooking time is finished, uncover the slow cooker and stir in parsley.
7) Serve hot.

Ground Beef & Veggie Curry

Cook time: 5¼ hours | Serves: 4 | Per Serving: Calories 367, Carbs 30.8g, Fat 20.3g, Protein 16.1g

Ingredients:

- Coconut oil – 2 tbsp.
- Lean ground beef – 1 lb.
- Onion – 1, sliced
- Fresh ginger – 1 tsp. minced
- Garlic cloves – 3, minced
- Serrano pepper – 2, seeded and finely chopped
- Ground cumin – 1 tsp.
- Ground coriander – 1 tsp.
- Red pepper flakes – ½ tsp. crushed
- Red chili powder – ½ tsp.
- Ground turmeric – ¼ tsp.
- Tomatoes – 4, chopped
- Salt and ground black pepper, as required
- Carrot – 1, peeled and chopped
- Large potato 1, peeled and cubed
- Fresh peas – ½ C. Shelled
- Unsweetened coconut milk ½ C.
- Tomato sauce – ½ C.

Directions:

1) In a large-sized non-stick wok, heat 2 tbsp. of olive oil and cook beef for about 4-5 minutes.
2) Add onion and sauté for about 5 minutes.
3) Add ginger, garlic, Serrano and spices and sauté for about 1 minute.
4) Add tomatoes and cook for about 2-3 minutes, crushing with the back of a spoon.
5) Transfer the beef mixture into the pot of a slow cooker.
6) Add remaining ingredients and stir to combine.
7) Close the lid of the slow cooker and set on "Low" setting for 4-5 hours.
8) After cooking time is finished, uncover the slow cooker and serve hot.

Ground Beef with Quinoa

Cook time: 7¼ hours | Serves: 4 | Per Serving: Calories 479, Carbs 33.5g, Fat 12.6g, Protein 57.4g

Ingredients:

- Lean ground beef – 1½ lb.
- Garlic cloves – 2, minced
- Medium onion – 1, chopped
- Fresh mushroom – 1 C. finely chopped
- Carrots – 2, peeled and finely chopped
- Quinoa – ½ C. Rinsed
- Ketchup – ½ C.
- Tomato sauce 1 (8-oz.) can
- Applesauce – 2 tbsp.
- Red chili powder – ½ tbsp.
- Cayenne pepper – ½ tbsp.
- Ginger powder – 1 tsp.
- Water – 2 C.

Directions:

1) Heat a large non-stick wok over medium-high heat and cook beef and garlic for about 8-10 minutes.
2) With a slotted spoon, transfer the beef into the pot of a slow cooker.
3) In the same wok, add onion, mushroom and carrot over medium heat and cook for about 4-5 minutes.
4) Transfer the veggie mixture into the slow cooker.
5) Add remaining ingredients and stir to combine.
6) Close the lid of the slow cooker and set on "High" setting for 4 hours.
7) Now set the slow cooker on "Low" setting for 2-3 hours.
8) After cooking time is finished, uncover the slow cooker and serve hot.

Ground Beef with Pasta

Cook time: 8¾ hours | Serves: 4 | Per Serving: Calories 480, Carbs 53.4g, Fat 8.8g, Protein 45.6g

Ingredients:

- Lean ground beef – 1 lb.
- Garlic cloves – 4, minced
- Onion – 1, chopped
- Tomatoes – 1 C. chopped
- Tomato paste – ½ C.
- Fresh parsley – 1 tbsp. minced
- Salt and ground black pepper, as required
- Low-sodium beef broth – 2½ C.
- Uncooked whole-wheat pasta – 1¼ C.
- Water – 1 C.

Directions:

1) In the pot of a slow cooker, add all ingredients except for pasta and water and stir to combine.
2) Close the lid of the slow cooker and set on "Low" setting for 7-8 hours.
3) After cooking time is finished, uncover the slow cooker and stir in pasta and water.
4) Again, close the lid of the slow cooker and set on "High" setting for 40-45 minutes.
5) After cooking time is finished, uncover the slow cooker and serve hot.

Beef Cheeseburger Casserole

Cook time: 4 hours 10 minutes | Serves: 4 | Per Serving: Calories 586, Carbs 4g, Fat 45.4g, Protein 43.6g

Ingredients:

- Olive oil – 3 tbsp.
- Lean ground beef – 1 lb.
- Garlic cloves – 2, minced
- Red pepper flakes – ¼ tsp.
- Salt and ground black pepper, as required
- Cooked bacon slices – 4, chopped and divided
- Mexican cheese – 1½ C. shredded and divided
- Low-fat cream cheese – 4 oz. softened
- Large eggs – 6

Directions:

1) In a large-sized non-stick wok, heat the oil over medium heat and cook the ground beef for about 8-9 minutes or until browned.
2) Add the garlic, red pepper flakes, salt and black pepper and cook for about 1 minute.

3) Transfer the mixture into the pot of a slow cooker and spread in an even layer.
4) Sprinkle with ¾ of the bacon bits and 1 C. of the shredded cheese.
5) In a large-sized bowl, add the cream cheese and eggs and beat until smooth.
6) Place the egg mixture over the beef mixture.
7) Close the lid of the slow cooker and set on "Low" setting for 4 hours.
8) After cooking time is finished, uncover the slow cooker and sprinkle the top with the remaining cheese.
9) Immediately close the pot with its lid for about 10 minutes before serving.
10) Serve with the sprinkling of remaining bacon.

Ground Beef & Eggplant Casserole

Cook time: 3 hours 10 minutes │Serves: 4 │ Per Serving: Calories 309, Carbs 9.2g, Fat 20.6g, Protein 23.4g

Ingredients:

- Eggplant – 1 C. cubed
- Salt, as required
- Olive oil – ½ tbsp.
- Lean ground beef – 1 lb.
- Worcestershire sauce – 1 tsp.
- Dijon mustard – 1 tsp.
- Ground black pepper, as required
- Diced tomatoes – 1 (14-oz.) can, drained
- Tomato sauce – 8 oz.
- Mozzarella cheese – 1 C. grated
- Fresh parsley – 1 tbsp. chopped
- Dried oregano – 1 tsp.

Directions:

1) In a colander, place the eggplant and sprinkle with salt.
2) Set aside for about 30 minutes.
3) Heat a non-stick wok over a medium heat and cook the ground beef for about 8-10 minutes or until browned.
4) Drain the grease and transfer the beef into a bowl.
5) Transfer the eggplant into a bowl and mix with olive oil.
6) In the bowl of beef, add Worcestershire sauce, mustard, salt and black pepper and mix well.
7) Lightly grease the pot of a slow cooker.
8) In the greased pot, place the beef mixture and top with eggplant.
9) Spread tomatoes and sauce over eggplant and sprinkle with cheese, followed by parsley and oregano.
10) Close the lid of the slow cooker and set on "High" setting for 3 hours.
11) After cooking time is finished, uncover the slow cooker and serve hot.

Beef Meatloaf

Cook time: 6 hours | Serves: 4 | Per Serving: Calories 308, Carbs 8.8g, Fat 21.2g, Protein 15.6g

Ingredients:

- Medium onion – 1, minced
- Garlic cloves – 3, minced
- Lean ground beef – 1½ lb.
- Almond flour – ¾ C.
- Mozzarella cheese – 1 C. shredded
- Large eggs – 2
- Worcestershire sauce – 2 tsp.
- Salt and ground black pepper, as required
- Tomato sauce – ¼ C.

Directions:

1) Lightly grease the pot of a slow cooker.
2) In a large-sized bowl, add all ingredients except for the tomato sauce and mix well until blended.
3) In the greased pot of the slow cooker, place the beef mixture and shape into an oval.
4) Cover the meatloaf with tomato sauce.
5) Close the lid of the slow cooker and set on "Low" setting for 6 hours.
6) After the cooking time is finished, uncover the slow cooker and transfer the meatloaf onto a cutting board.
7) Cut the meatloaf into desired-sized slices and serve.

Cheesy Beef Lasagna

Cook time: 6 hours 10 minutes | Serves: 4 | Per Serving: Calories 448, Carbs 32.1g, Fat 15.2g, Protein 43.7g

Ingredients:

- Lean ground beef – ¾ lb.
- Small onion – 1, chopped
- Pasta sauce – 12 oz.
- Fresh basil leaves – 3, chopped
- Salt, as required
- Mozzarella cheese – 1 C. shredded and divided
- Parmesan cheese – ½ C. shredded
- Part-skim ricotta cheese – 8 oz.
- Uncooked lasagna noodles – 8

Directions:

1) Heat a non-stick wok over a medium heat and cook the beef and onion for about 8-10 minutes.
2) Drain the grease from the wok.
3) In the wok, add the pasta sauce, basil and salt and stir to combine.

4) Remove from the heat and set aside.
5) In a bowl, add 1 C. of the mozzarella, Parmesan and ricotta cheese and mix.
6) In the pot of a slow cooker, place ¼ of the beef mixture evenly and arrange 5 noodles on top, breaking them to fit in the pot.
7) Place half of the cheese mixture on top of the noodles.
8) Repeat the layer twice, ending with ¼ of the beef mixture.
9) Close the lid of the slow cooker and set on "Low" setting for 4-6 hours.
10) In the last 20 minutes of cooking, sprinkle the lasagna with the remaining mozzarella cheese.
11) After cooking time is finished, uncover the slow cooker and serve hot.

Beef Meatballs in BBQ Sauce

Cook time: 3 hours 5 minutes │Serves: 4 │ Per Serving: Calories 465, Carbs 14.2g, Fat 21.6g, Protein 51.5g

Ingredients:

- Lean ground beef – 1¼ lb.
- Mozzarella cheese – ½ C. shredded
- Parmesan cheese – ½ C. grated
- Eggs – 2
- Coconut flour – 2 tbsp.
- Onion – ¾ tsp. minced
- Italian seasoning – ¼ tsp.
- Garlic powder – ¼ tsp.
- Salt and ground black pepper, as required
- Olive oil – 2 tbsp.
- BBQ sauce – ½ C.
- Low-sodium beef broth – 1/3 C.

Directions:

1) In a large-sized bowl, add all ingredients except for the oil, BBQ sauce and broth and mix well blended.
2) Make equal-sized balls from the mixture.
3) In a non-stick wok, heat oil over medium heat and cook the meatballs for about 4-5 minutes or until browned complexly.
4) Transfer the meatballs into the pot of a slow cooker and top with BBQ sauce and broth.
5) Close the lid of the slow cooker and set on "High" setting for 3 hours.
6) After cooking time is finished, uncover the slow cooker and serve hot.

Beef Meatballs with Spaghetti Sauce

Cook time: 4¾ hours | Serves: 4 | Per Serving: Calories 549, Carbs 64.6g, Fat 17g, Protein 37.1g

Ingredients:

For Meatballs:

- Lean ground beef – 1 lb.
- Fresh parsley – ¼ C. minced
- Plain breadcrumbs – ¼ C.
- Olive oil – 1 tbsp.
- Ground allspice – ½ tsp.
- Ground cinnamon – ½ tsp.
- Ground cumin – ½ tsp.
- Cayenne pepper – ¼ tsp.
- Salt and ground black pepper, as required

For Sauce:

- Crushed tomatoes – 1 (28-oz.) can
- Diced tomatoes – 1 (15-oz.) can
- Tomato sauce – 1 (15-oz.) can
- Low-sodium beef broth – 1 C.
- Medium sweet onion – ½, chopped
- Garlic cloves – 3, minced
- Granulated sugar– 2 tsp.
- Salt and ground black pepper, as required
- Whole-wheat spaghetti– 8 oz. broken in half

Directions:

1) For meatballs: in a large-sized bowl, add all ingredients except for oil and mix well until blended.
2) Make equal-sized balls from the mixture.
3) In a large-sized non-stick wok over a medium-high heat, cook the meatballs for about 4-5 minutes or until browned.
4) Transfer the meatballs onto a paper towel-lined plate.
5) For sauce: in the pot of a slow cooker, add all ingredients except for spaghetti and basil and stir to combine.
6) Add the meatballs and gently stir.
7) Close the lid of the slow cooker and set on "High" setting for 3-4 hours.
8) After cooking time is finished, uncover the slow cooker and stir in the spaghetti pieces.
9) Close the lid of the slow cooker and set on "Low" setting for 40 minutes.
10) While cooking, stir the mixture once halfway through.
11) After cooking time is finished, uncover the slow cooker and serve hot.

Pork Recipes

Herbed Pork Loin

Cook time: 8 hours | Serves: 4 | Per Serving: Calories 423, Carbs 1.9g, Fat 23.8g, Protein 47.2g

Ingredients:

- Olive oil – 2 tbsp.
- Low-sodium chicken broth – ¾ C.
- Paprika – ½ tbsp.
- Garlic powder – ½ tbsp.
- Dried sage – ½ tsp.
- Dried basil – ½ tsp.
- Dried oregano – ½ tsp.
- Dried marjoram – ¼ tsp.
- Dried rosemary – ¼ tsp.
- Dried thyme – ¼ tsp.
- Boneless pork loin – 1½ lb. trimmed

Directions:

1) In a small-sized bowl, add all the ingredients except for pork loin and mix well.
2) In the bottom of a slow cooker, place the pork loin and top with the oil mixture.
3) Close the lid of the slow cooker and set on "Low" setting for 7-8 hours.
4) After cooking time is finished, uncover the slow cooker and place the pork loin onto a cutting board.
5) Cut into desired-sized slices and serve.

Spiced Pork Shoulder

Cook time: 8 hours | Serves: 4 | Per Serving: Calories 311, Carbs 1.4g, Fat 13.1g, Protein 44.8g

Ingredients:

- Olive oil – 2 tbsp.
- Fresh lemon juice – 2 tbsp.
- Red wine vinegar – 1 tbsp.
- Dried oregano – ½ tbsp.
- Dried mint – ½ tbsp.
- Za'atar – ½ tbsp.
- Garlic powder – ½ tbsp.
- Chili flakes – 1 tsp.
- Salt, as required
- Boneless pork shoulder – 1½ lb. trimmed

Directions:

1) In a small-sized bowl, add all ingredients except for pork shoulder and mix well.
2) In the pot of a slow cooker, place the pork shoulder and top with the oil mixture
3) Close the lid of the slow cooker and set on "Low" setting for 8 hours.
4) After cooking time is finished, uncover the slow cooker and transfer the pork shoulder onto a cutting board.
5) Cut into desired-sized slices and serve.

BBQ Pork Ribs

Cook time: 4¼ hours │Serves: 4 │ Per Serving: Calories 571, Carbs 69.7g, Fat 21.4g, Protein 30.3g

Ingredients:

- Baby back ribs – 2 lb. trimmed
- Salt and ground black pepper, as required
- Water – ½ C.
- Onion – ½, sliced
- Garlic clove – 1, minced
- BBQ sauce – 14 oz.

Directions:

1) Rub the ribs with salt and black pepper generously.
2) In the pot of a slow cooker, pour the water.
3) Arrange the ribs in water and top with onion and garlic.
4) Close the lid of the slow cooker and set on "High" setting for 4 hours.
5) Meanwhile, preheat your oven to 375 °F.
6) After cooking time is finished, uncover the slow cooker and discard onion and garlic.
7) Transfer the ribs onto a baking sheet.
8) Coat the ribs with BBQ sauce evenly.
9) Bake for approximately 10-15 minutes.
10) Serve hot.

Glazed Pork Ribs

Cook time: 5 hours | Serves: 4 | Per Serving: Calories 803, Carbs 26.3g, Fat 60.2g, Protein 38g

Ingredients:

- Fresh ginger – 2 tbsp. minced
- Garlic – 1 tbsp. minced
- Chili sauce – 1/3 C.
- Low-sodium soy sauce – 1/3 C.
- Honey – ¼ C.
- Balsamic vinegar – ¼ C.
- Sesame oil – 2 tbsp.
- Brown sugar – 2 tbsp.
- Ground black pepper, as required
- Pork baby back ribs – 2 lb. trimmed

Directions:

1) In a small-sized bowl, add all ingredients except for ribs and mix well.
2) In the pot of a slow cooker, arrange the ribs and top with honey mixture.
3) Close the lid of the slow cooker and set on "High" setting for 4½-5 hours.
4) After cooking time is finished, uncover the slow cooker and serve hot.

BBQ Pork Chops

Cook time: 2 hours 35 minutes | Serves: 4 | Per Serving: Calories 238, Carbs 10.6g, Fat 1g, Protein 7.9g

Ingredients:

- Dried rosemary – 1 tsp.
- Onion powder – 1 tsp.
- Garlic powder – 1 tsp.
- Salt and ground black pepper, as required
- Boneless chops pork chops – 4 (6-oz.)
- BBQ sauce – 2 C.
- Small yellow onion – 1 thinly sliced
- Cornstarch – 2 tbsp.
- Water – 2 tbsp.

Directions:

1) Grease the pot of a slow cooker.
2) In a small bowl, blend together the rosemary, onion powder, garlic powder, salt and pepper.
3) Rub the pork chops with rosemary mixture evenly.
4) In the pot of greased slow cooker, spread a thin layer of BBQ sauce.
5) Arrange the onion slices over the sauce evenly.
6) Now place the chops over the onion slices and top with the remaining BBQ sauce.
7) Close the lid of the slow cooker and set on "Low" setting for 2-2½ hours.

8) After cooking time is finished, uncover the slow cooker and with tongs, transfer the chops onto a plate.
9) With a piece of foil cover the chops to keep warm.
10) In a small-sized bowl, whisk together the cornstarch and water.
11) Transfer the pot sauce into a medium-sized saucepan over medium heat.
12) Whisk in the cornstarch mixture and cook for about 5-10 minutes, stirring continuously.
13) Pour the sauce over chops and serve.

Pork Chops in Creamy Sauce

Cook time: 7 hours 5 minutes │Serves: 4 │ Per Serving: Calories 288, Carbs 13.9g, Fat 14.7g, Protein 25.7g

Ingredients:

- Ranch dressing mix – 1 envelope
- Garlic powder – ½ tsp.
- Ground black pepper, as required
- Boneless pork chops – 1 lb.
- Cream of chicken soup – 1 (10½-oz.) can
- Low-sodium beef broth – 1½ C.
- Brown gravy mix – 1 envelope
- Cornstarch – 2 tbsp.
- Water – 2 tbsp.

Directions:

1) In a small-sized bowl, blend together the ranch dressing mix, garlic powder, and pepper.
2) Season both sides of the pork chops with dressing mixture.
3) In the pot of a slow cooker, whisk together the cream of chicken soup, broth and brown gravy mix.
4) Place the chop in the pot and gently stir with the soup mixture.
5) Close the lid of the slow cooker and set on "Low" setting for 6-7 hours.
6) After cooking time is finished, uncover the slow cooker and with tongs, transfer the chops onto a plate.
7) With a piece of foil cover the chops to keep warm.
8) In a small-sized bowl, whisk together the cornstarch and water.
9) Transfer the pot sauce into a medium-sized saucepan over a medium heat.
10) Whisk in the cornstarch mixture and cook for about 5 minutes, stirring continuously.
11) Add in the chops and remove the pan from heat.
12) Serve hot.

Teriyaki Pulled Pork

Cook time: 4 hours | Serves: 4 | Per Serving: Calories 289, Carbs 9.4g, Fat 6g, Protein 46.5g

Ingredients:

not great

- Teriyaki sauce – 1/3 C.
- Low-sodium chicken broth – ¾ C.
- Brown sugar – 2 tbsp.
- Garlic cloves – 4, chopped
- Red chili peppers – 3, finely chopped
- Ground black pepper – ¼ tsp.
- Pork tenderloin – 1½ lb. trimmed

Directions:

1) In a medium-sized bowl, add all ingredients and mix well.
2) In the pot of a slow cooker, place the pork tenderloin and top with sauce mixture.
3) Close the lid of the slow cooker and set on "High" setting for 4 hours
4) After cooking time is finished, uncover the slow cooker and with 2 forks, shred the meat.
5) Stir the shredded meat with pot sauce and serve hot.

Pineapple Pulled Pork

Cook time: 8 hours | Serves: 4 | Per Serving: Calories 415, Carbs 11.2g, Fat 27.8g, Protein 29.8g

Ingredients:

- Canned unsweetened crushed pineapple with juice – 10 oz.
- Minced garlic – 1 tbsp.
- Ground cumin – 1 tbsp.
- Red pepper flakes – 1 tsp.
- Salt and ground black pepper, as required
- Boneless pork butt roast – 1½ lb. trimmed

Directions:

1) In a medium-sized bowl, add all ingredients and mix well.
2) In the pot of a slow cooker, place the pork roast and top with pineapple mixture.
3) Close the lid of the slow cooker and set on "Low" setting for 8 hours
4) After cooking time is finished, uncover the slow cooker and with 2 forks, shred the meat.
5) Stir the shredded meat with pot sauce and serve hot.

Pork & Apple Curry

Cook time: 6½ hours | Serves: 4 | Per Serving: Calories 302, Carbs 24.8g, Fat 1g, Protein 38.2g

Ingredients:

- Boneless pork loin – 1¼ lb. trimmed and cut into 1-inch cubes
- Medium apple – 1, peeled, cored and chopped
- Small onion – 1, chopped
- Fresh orange juice – ½ C.
- Tomato paste – ¼ C.
- Curry powder – 1 tbsp.
- Garlic clove – 1, minced
- Ground ginger – ½ tsp.
- Ground cinnamon – ¼ tsp.
- Salt and ground black pepper, as required
- Cornstarch – 2 tbsp.
- Water – 2 tbsp.
- Raisins – ¼ C.

Directions:

1) In the pot of a slow cooker, add all ingredients except for cornstarch, water and raisins and mix well.
2) Close the lid of the slow cooker and set on "Low" setting for 6 hours.
3) Meanwhile, in a small-size bowl, whisk together the cornstarch and water.
4) After cooking time is finished, uncover the slow cooker and stir in the cornstarch mixture.
5) Again, close the lid of slow cooker and set on "High" setting for 30 minutes.
6) While cooking, stir the curry once halfway through.
7) After cooking time is finished, uncover the slow cooker and stir in the raisins.
8) Serve hot.

Pork & Tomato Curry

Cook time: 4 hours 10 minutes | Serves: 4 | Per Serving: Calories 456, Carbs 14g, Fat 26.8g, Protein 41.3g

Ingredients:

- Vegetable oil – 1 tbsp.
- Boneless pork shoulder – 1¼ lb. cut into 2-inch pieces
- Salt and ground black pepper, as required
- Large onion – 1, chopped
- Fresh ginger – 1 tbsp. minced
- Garlic cloves – 2, minced
- Curry powder – 1 tbsp.

- Ground cumin – 1 tsp.
- Diced tomatoes with juices – 1 (14-oz.) can
- Unsweetened coconut milk – 1 C.
- Low-sodium chicken broth – 2 C.

Directions:

1) In a large-sized wok, heat oil over medium-high heat and sear the pork pieces with salt and black pepper for about 4-5 minutes.
2) With a slotted spoon, transfer the pork pieces into the pot of a slow cooker.
3) In the same wok, add onion, ginger, garlic, curry powder and cumin over a medium-low heat and cook for about 5 minutes.
4) Transfer the onion mixture into the slow cooker.
5) Add the tomatoes, coconut milk and broth and stir to combine.
6) Close the lid of the slow cooker and set on "High" setting for 4 hours.
7) After cooking time is finished, uncover the slow cooker serve hot.

Pork & Potato Curry

Cook time: 5 hours | Serves: 4 | Per Serving: Calories 331, Carbs 17.3g, Fat 15.1g, Protein 43.9g

Ingredients:

- Boneless pork loin 1 lb. trimmed and cut into 1-inch cubes
- Potato – 1, cut into 1-inch cubes
- Onion – ½ C. chopped
- Bell pepper – ½ C. seeded and chopped
- Garlic – ½ tbsp. minced
- Fresh ginger – ½ tbsp. grated
- Tomato paste – ¼ C.
- Water – ¼ C.
- Curry powder – ½ tbsp.
- Salt and ground black pepper, as required
- Unsweetened coconut milk – ¾ C.

Directions:

1) In the pot of a slow cooker, add all ingredients except for coconut milk and stir to combine.
2) Close the lid of the slow cooker and set on "Low" setting for 5 hours.
3) After cooking time is finished, uncover the slow cooker and immediately stir in coconut milk.
4) Serve hot.

Pork & Chickpea Curry

Cook time: 8 hours | Serves: 4 | Per Serving: Calories 388, Carbs 32.3g, Fat 12.8g, Protein 37.3g

Ingredients:

- Boneless pork loin – 1 lb. trimmed and cut into cubes
- Diced tomatoes with juices – 1 (14-oz.) can
- Brown onion – 1, sliced
- Curry powder – 1 tbsp.
- Fresh baby spinach – 3 C.
- Chickpeas – 1 (14-oz.) can, rinsed and drained
- Unsweetened coconut milk – ½ C.

Directions:

1) In the pot of a slow cooker, add pork cubes, tomatoes, onion and curry powder and stir to combine.
2) Close the lid of the slow cooker and set on "Low" setting for 7-7½ hours.
3) After cooking time is finished, uncover the slow cooker and immediately stir in spinach, chickpeas and coconut milk.
4) Again, close the lid of the slow cooker and set on "High" setting for 30 minutes.
5) After cooking time is finished, uncover the slow cooker and serve hot.

Pork with Cranberries

Cook time: 8 hours | Serves: 4 | Per Serving: Calories 252, Carbs 17.6g, Fat 4.8g, Protein 34.3g

Ingredients:

- Boneless pork meat – 1½ lb. trimmed and cubed
- Salt and ground black pepper, as required
- Tomato paste – ¾ C.
- Medium onion – 1, finely chopped
- Dried unsweetened cranberries – ¾ C.

Directions:

1) Sprinkle the pork cubes with salt and black pepper evenly.
2) Heat a greased wok over a medium heat and sear the pork cubes for about 4-5 minutes or until browned completely.
3) Transfer the pork cubes into a slow cooker.
4) Add the remaining ingredients and stir to combine.
5) Close the lid of the slow cooker and set on "Low" setting for 8 hours.

6) After cooking time is finished, uncover the slow cooker and serve hot.

Pork with Apple

Cook time: 5 hours | Serves: 4 | Per Serving: Calories 224, Carbs 16g, Fat 4.3g, Protein 30.5g

Ingredients:

- Apples – 2, cored and sliced
- Pork tenderloin – 1 lb. trimmed
- Ground nutmeg – ½ tsp.
- Low-sodium soy sauce – ¼ C.

Directions:

1) Lightly grease the pot of a slow cooker.
2) Place half of the apple slices in the prepared slow cooker pot.
3) With a sharp knife, make slits into the pork.
4) Place the pork tenderloin over the apple slices and sprinkle with half of the nutmeg.
5) Place the remaining apple slices over pork tenderloin and sprinkle with the remaining nutmeg.
6) Pour soy sauce on top.
7) Close the lid of the slow cooker and set on "Low" setting for 5 hours.
8) After cooking time is finished, uncover the slow cooker and transfer the pork onto a cutting board.
9) Cut the pork into bite-sized pieces and stir with apple mixture.
10) Serve immediately.

Pork with Pineapple

Cook time: 8¼ hours | Serves: 4 | Per Serving: Calories 321, Carbs 18.8g, Fat 6.1g, Protein 45.9g

Ingredients:

- Boneless pork loin – 1½ lb. cut into cubes
- Pineapple tidbits in unsweetened juice – 1 (8-oz.) can, undrained
- Medium bell pepper – 1, seeded and cut into squares
- Brown sugar – 2 tbsp.
- Ground ginger – ½ tsp.
- White vinegar – ¼ C.
- Low-sodium soy sauce – 3 tbsp.
- Cornstarch – 2 tbsp.
- Water – 3 tbsp.

Directions:

1) In the pot of a slow cooker, place all the ingredients except for cornstarch and water and stir to combine.
2) Close the lid of the slow cooker and set on "Low" setting for 6-8 hours.
3) Meanwhile, in a small-sized bowl, whisk together the cornstarch and water.
4) After cooking time is finished, uncover the slow cooker and stir in the cornstarch mixture.
5) Again, close the lid of the slow cooker and set on "High" setting for 10-15 minutes.
6) After cooking time is finished, uncover the slow cooker and serve hot.

Pork with Spinach

Cook time: 8 hours 25 minutes | Serves: 4 | Per Serving: Calories 278, Carbs 4.1g, Fat 11.1g, Protein 39.1g

Ingredients:

- Unsalted butter – 2 tbsp.
- Small onion – 1, chopped
- Garlic cloves – 2, minced
- Ground cumin – 1 tsp.
- Ground turmeric – ½ tsp.
- Cayenne pepper – ½ tsp.
- Low-sodium chicken broth – 1¼ C.
- Boneless pork – 1¼ lb. trimmed and cubed
- Salt and ground black pepper, as required
- Fresh baby spinach – 4 C.

Directions:

1) In a large-sized wok, melt butter over a medium-high heat and sauté onion for about 4 minutes.
2) Add garlic and spices and sauté for 1 minute.
3) Add broth and bring to a boil, stirring once.
4) Remove the wok broth mixture from heat.
5) In the pot of a slow cooker, place pork cubes and sprinkle with salt and black pepper.
6) Pour the broth mixture on top.
7) Close the lid of the slow cooker and set on "Low" setting for 8 hours.
8) After cooking time is finished, uncover the slow cooker and stir in baby spinach.
9) Again, close the lid of the slow cooker and set on "High" setting for 10-15 minutes.
10) After cooking time is finished, uncover the slow cooker and serve hot.

Pork with Potatoes

Cook time: 6 hours |Serves: 4 | Per Serving: Calories 490, Carbs 15.1g, Fat 26.9g, Protein 40.4g

Ingredients:

- Pork loin – 1¼ lb. rolled
- Garlic cloves – 3, sliced thinly
- Fresh rosemary bunch – 1
- Olive oil – 2 tbsp.
- Potatoes – 1 lb. peeled and cubed
- Dry white wine – ½ C.
- Fresh lemon juice – 2 tbsp.

Directions:

1) With a sharp knife, cut slits into the pork on both sides.
2) Insert 1 garlic slice in each slit.
3) In a large wok, heat oil over a medium-high heat and sear the pork loin for about 4-5 minutes or until browned from all sides.
4) Remove from the heat and insert the rosemary into the slits with the garlic.
5) In the pot of a slow cooker, place the potatoes, followed by 2 rosemary stalks and pork loin.
6) Place the wine and lemon juice on top.
7) Close the lid of the slow cooker and set on "Low" setting for 6 hours.
8) After cooking time is finished, uncover the slow cooker and with a slotted spoon, transfer the pork loin onto a platter.
9) Cut the pork loin into desired sized slices and serve alongside the potatoes.

Pork with Eggplant

Cook time: 4 hours |Serves: 4 | Per Serving: Calories 193, Carbs 6.3g, Fat 4.1g, Protein 31.3g

Ingredients:

- Yellow onion – 1, sliced
- Pork tenderloin – 1 lb. cut into slices
- Eggplant – ½ lb. cubed
- Salt and ground black pepper, as required
- Low-sodium chicken broth – 1½ C.

Directions:

1) Grease the pot of a slow cooker generously.
2) In the pot, arrange the onion slices and top with the pork tenderloin, followed by the eggplant cubes.
3) Sprinkle with salt and black pepper and pour the broth on top.
4) Close the lid of the slow cooker and set on "High" setting for 4 hours.
5) After cooking time is finished, uncover the slow cooker and serve hot.

Pork with Carrots

Cook time: 8 hours | Serves: 4 | Per Serving: Calories 458, Carbs 5g, Fat 34.7g, Protein 29.1g

Ingredients:

- Boneless pork shoulder roast – 1½ lb. trimmed
- Dried basil – 1 tsp. crushed
- Dried oregano – 1 tsp. crushed
- Dried thyme – 1 tsp. crushed
- Salt and ground black pepper, as required
- Small onion – 1, sliced thinly
- Medium carrots– 2, peeled and sliced lengthwise

Directions:

1) In a large-sized bowl, place the pork shoulder.
2) Rub the pork shoulder with dried herbs, salt and black pepper generously.
3) Cover the bowl and set aside for at least 3-4 hours.
4) In the pot of a slow cooker, place onion and carrots and sprinkle with salt and pepper.
5) Place the pork shoulder over carrots.
6) Close the lid of the slow cooker and set on "Low" setting for 8-10 hours.
7) After cooking time is finished, uncover the slow cooker and with tongs, transfer the pork shoulder onto a cutting board.
8) Cut the pork into bite-sized pieces.
9) Add the pork pieces into the pot and mix well.
10) Serve immediately.

Pork with Beans

Cook time: 10 hours 10 minutes | Serves: 4 | Per Serving: Calories 653, Carbs 61.4g, Fat 15.4g, Protein 65.4g

Ingredients:

- BBQ sauce – ¾ C.
- Chipotle in adobo – 1, finely chopped
- Light brown sugar – 2 tbsp.
- Boneless pork shoulder – 1½ lb. trimmed
- Salt and ground black pepper, as required
- Olive oil – 1 tbsp.
- Pinto beans – 1½ (14-oz.) cans, rinsed and drained
- Garlic cloves – 4, thinly sliced

Directions:

1) In the pot of a slow cooker, blend together the BBQ sauce, chipotle and brown sugar.
2) Rub the pork shoulder with salt and black pepper evenly.
3) In a large-sized non-stick wok, heat oil medium-high heat and cook the pork shoulder for about 8-10 minutes or until browned on all sides.
4) Transfer the pork into the slow cooker with the sauce and mix well.
5) Top with beans and garlic slices.
6) Close the lid of the slow cooker and set on "Low" setting for 8-10 hours.
7) After cooking time is finished, uncover the slow cooker and with tongs, transfer the pork shoulder onto a cutting board.
8) Cut the pork into bite-sized pieces.
9) Add the pork pieces into the pot and mix well.
10) Serve immediately.

Pork Chops with Tomatoes

Cook time: 8 hours | Serves: 4 | Per Serving: Calories 179, Carbs 3.1g, Fat 4.1g, Protein 30.8g

Ingredients:

- Pork chops – 1 lb.
- Tomatoes – 1½ C. finely chopped
- Low-sodium chicken broth – 1 C.
- Dried mixed herbs (oregano, thyme, sage) – 1 tbsp.
- Salt and ground black pepper, as required

Directions:

1) In the pot of a slow cooker, add all ingredients and mix.
2) Close the lid of slow cooker and set on "Low" setting for 8 hours.
3) After cooking time is finished, uncover the slow cooker and serve hot.

Pork Chops with Artichokes & Peas

Cook time: 6 hours | Serves: 4 | Per Serving: Calories 357, Carbs 15.6g, Fat 13.5g, Protein 33.6g

Ingredients:

- Dry white wine – 1 C.
- Unsalted butter – 2 tbsp. melted
- Tomato paste – 2 tbsp.
- Boneless pork chops – 1 lb.
- Fresh thyme – 1 tbsp. chopped
- Salt and ground black pepper, as required
- Extra-virgin olive oil – 1 tbsp.
- Large onion – 1, sliced thinly
- Marinated artichokes – 10 oz. drained
- Frozen green peas – ½ C.

Directions:

1) In a small-sized bowl, add the wine, butter and tomato paste and beat well until blended. Set aside.
2) Rub the chops with thyme, salt and black pepper evenly.
3) In a non-stick wok, heat the oil over a medium-high heat and sear the chops for about 4-5 minutes or until browned completely.
4) Remove from the heat and place the chops in the pot of a slow cooker.
5) Place onion slices over the chops and top with wine mixture, followed by artichokes.
6) Close the lid of the slow cooker and set on "Low" setting for 5½ hours.
7) After cooking time is finished, uncover the slow cooker and stir in the peas.
8) Close the lid of the slow cooker and set on "Low" setting for 30 minutes.
9) After cooking time is finished, uncover the slow cooker and serve hot.

Pork Chops with Zucchini

Cook time: 5½ hours | Serves: 4 | Per Serving: Calories 208, Carbs 3.5g, Fat 7.6g, Protein 30.8g

Ingredients:

- Coconut oil – 1 tbsp.
- Garlic cloves – 2, minced
- Boneless pork chops – 4 (4-oz.)
- Salt and ground black pepper, as required
- Large zucchini – 1, cubed
- Lemons – 2, sliced
- Red pepper flakes – 1 tsp. crushed

Directions:

1) In a large-sized wok, heat oil over a medium-high heat and sauté the garlic for about 1 minute.
2) Add the chops and cook for about 1-2 minutes per side.
3) Transfer the chops mixture into a slow cooker.
4) Place cubed zucchini over chops evenly and sprinkle with salt and black pepper.
5) Close the lid of the slow cooker and set on "Low" setting for 5-5½ hours.
6) After cooking time is finished, uncover the slow cooker and serve.

Pork Ribs with Green Beans

Cook time: 6½ hours | Serves: 4 | Per Serving: Calories 238, Carbs 8.2g, Fat 5.1g, Protein 38.2g

Ingredients:

- Dried onion flakes – 2 tbsp.
- Parsley flakes – ¼ tsp.
- Salt and ground black pepper, as required
- Country-style boneless pork ribs – 1¼ lb. cut into strips
- Water – ½ C.
- Fresh green beans – ¾ lb. trimmed and chopped

Directions:

1) In a small-sized bowl, add onion flakes, parsley flakes, salt and black pepper and mix well.
2) In the pot of a slow cooker, place the ribs and top with spice mixture, followed by water.
3) Close the lid of the slow cooker and set on "Low" setting for 6 hours.
4) After cooking time is finished, uncover the slow cooker and stir in the green beans.
5) Again, close the lid of the slow cooker and set on "High" setting for 30 minutes.
6) After cooking time is finished, uncover the slow cooker and serve hot.

Pork Chops with Mushroom Sauce

Cook time: 4 hours | Serves: 4 | Per Serving: Calories 319, Carbs 10.5g, Fat 11.4g, Protein 41.7g

Ingredients:

- Cream of mushroom soup – 1 (10-oz.) can
- Cream of chicken soup – 1 (10-oz.) can
- Low-sodium beef broth – ½ C.
- Garlic – 2 tsp. minced
- Paprika – 1 tsp.
- Ground black pepper, as required
- Boneless pork chops – 4 (5-oz.)
- Fresh mushrooms – 8 oz. sliced
- Onion – ½, sliced

Directions:

1) In a large-sized bowl, whisk together the cream soups, broth, garlic, paprika and black pepper.
2) In the pot of a slow cooker, place the chops and top with mushrooms and onion slices.
3) Pour the broth mixture on top evenly.
4) Close the lid of the slow cooker and set on "High" setting for 3-4 hours
5) After cooking time is finished, uncover the slow cooker and serve hot.

Pork & Apricot Casserole

Cook time: 6 hours | Serves: 4 | Per Serving: Calories 377, Carbs 26.6g, Fat 19.4g, Protein 26.3g

Ingredients:

- Ground cumin – 1 tsp.
- Ground coriander – 1 tsp.
- Ground cinnamon – 1 tsp.
- Boneless pork meat – 1 lb. trimmed and cubed
- Olive oil – 1 tbsp.
- Tomato paste – 1½ C.
- Medium onion – 1, finely chopped
- Garlic cloves – 2, minced
- Dried apricots – 1 C.

Directions:

1) In a large-sized bowl, blend together the spices.
2) Add the pork cubes and coat with the spice mixture evenly.
3) In a large-sized non-stick wok, heat oil over a medium heat and cook the pork cubes for about 3-5 minutes or until browned completely.
4) Transfer the pork cubes into the pot of a slow cooker with the remaining ingredients and stir to combine.
5) Close the lid of the slow cooker and set on "Low" setting for 6-8 hours.
6) After cooking time is finished, uncover the slow cooker and serve hot.

Ground Pork with Olives

Cook time: 4 hours 10 minutes | Serves: 4 | Per Serving: Calories 3958, Carbs 7.1g, Fat 27.9g, Protein 30.3g

Ingredients:

- Olive oil – 1 tsp.
- Lean ground pork – 1½ lb.
- Bell peppers – ½ C. seeded and chopped
- Onion – ½ C. minced
- Garlic cloves – 2, minced
- Fresh cilantro – 2 tbsp. minced
- Small tomato – 1, chopped
- Tomato sauce – 6 oz.
- Green olives – ¼ C. pitted
- Bay leaf – 1
- Ground cumin – 1 tsp.
- Garlic powder – ¼ tsp.
- Salt and ground black pepper, as required
- Water – 1 C.

Directions:

1) In a non-stick wok, heat oil over medium-high heat and cook the pork with salt and black pepper for about 5-6 minutes.
2) Add the bell peppers, onion and garlic and cook for about 3-4 minutes.
3) Transfer the pork mixture into the pot of a slow cooker.
4) In the pot, add remaining ingredients and stir to combine.

5) Close the lid of the slow cooker and set on "High" setting for 4 hours.
6) After cooking time is finished, uncover the slow cooker and discard the bay leaf.
7) Serve hot.

Pork Meatballs in Tomato Sauce

Cook time: 6 hours 2 minutes | Serves: 4 | Per Serving: Calories 445, Carbs 22.3g, Fat 25.1g, Protein 33.5g

Ingredients:

For Meatballs:

- Lean ground pork – 1¼ lb.
- Egg – 1
- Parmigiano Reggiano cheese – ¼ C. grated
- Whole-wheat seasoned breadcrumbs – ¼ C.
- Fresh parsley – ¼ C. finely chopped
- Garlic clove – 1, minced
- Salt, as required

For Sauce:

- Olive oil – 1 tsp.
- Garlic cloves – 4, smashed
- Crushed tomatoes – 1 (28-oz.) can
- Bay leaf – 1
- Salt and ground black pepper, as required
- Fresh basil – ¼ C. minced

Directions:

1) For meatballs: in a large-sized bowl, add all ingredients and mix well until blended.
2) Make small equal-sized balls from the mixture.
3) For sauce: in a small-sized wok, heat olive oil over a medium heat and sauté the garlic for about 1 minute.
4) Stir in the tomatoes, bay leaf, salt and black pepper and remove from heat.
5) In the pot of a slow cooker, place the meatballs and top with the sauce.
6) Close the lid of the slow cooker and set on "Low" setting for 4-6 hours
7) After cooking time is finished, uncover the slow cooker and serve hot with the garnishing of basil.

Sausage with Bell Peppers

Cook time: 6 hours | Serves: 4 | Per Serving: Calories 234, Carbs 15.2g, Fat 11.6g, Protein 18.7g

Ingredients:

- Pork sausage – 1 lb. sliced
- Medium bell peppers – 2, seeded and sliced
- Tomatoes – 2 C. finely chopped
- Medium onion – 1, sliced
- Garlic powder – 2 tsp.
- Ground black pepper, as required

Directions:

1) In the pot of a slow cooker add all ingredients and stir to combine.
2) Close the lid of the slow cooker and set on "Low" setting for 6 hours.
3) After cooking time is finished, uncover the slow cooker and serve hot.

Sausage & Veggie Pie

Cook time: 8 hours | Serves: 4 | Per Serving: Calories 232, Carbs 11.9g, Fat 13.6g, Protein 16.1g

Ingredients:

- Pork sausage – 1 lb. chopped
- Sweet potato – 1, peeled and shredded
- Large bell pepper – 1, seeded and chopped
- Onion – 1, chopped
- Eggs – 8, beaten
- Fresh basil – 2 tsp. chopped
- Garlic powder – 1 tsp.
- Ground black pepper, as required

Directions:

1) In the pot of a slow cooker, add all ingredients and stir to combine.
2) Close the lid of the slow cooker and set on "Low" setting for 6-8 hours.
3) After cooking time is finished, uncover the slow cooker and serve warm.

Fish & Seafood Recipes

Salmon in Dill Sauce

Cook time: 2 hours | Serves: 4 | Per Serving: Calories 165, Carbs 2.4g, Fat 7.3g, Protein 23.2g

Ingredients:

- Water – 1½ C.
- Low-sodium chicken broth – 1 C.
- Fresh lemon juice – 2 tbsp.
- Fresh dill – ¼ C. chopped
- Lemon zest – ½ tsp. grated
- Salmon fillets – 4 (4-oz.)
- Cayenne pepper – 1 tsp.
- Salt and ground black pepper, as required

Directions:

1) In the pot of a slow cooker, blend together the water, broth, lemon juice, lemon juice, dill and lemon zest.
2) Arrange the salmon fillets on top, skin side down and sprinkle with cayenne pepper, salt and black pepper.
3) Close the lid of the slow cooker and set on "Low" setting for 1-2 hours.
4) After cooking time is finished, uncover the slow cooker and serve hot.

Salmon with Lemon Sauce

Cook time: 2 hours 8 minutes | Serves: 4 | Per Serving: Calories 315, Carbs 2.2g, Fat 18.1g, Protein 34.2g

Ingredients:

For Salmon:

- Italian seasoning – 1 tsp.
- Garlic powder – 1 tsp.
- Red chili powder – ½ tsp.
- Sweet paprika – ½ tsp.
- Salt and ground black pepper, as required
- Skin-on salmon fillet – 1½ lb.
- Olive oil cooking spray
- Lemon – 1, cut into slices
- Low-sodium chicken broth – 1 C.
- Fresh lemon juice – 2 tbsp.

For Lemon Sauce:

- Heavy cream – 2/3 C.
- White wine – ¼ C.
- Fresh lemon juice – 2 tbsp.
- Lemon zest – 1/8 tsp. grated finely
- Fresh parsley – 2 tbsp. chopped

Directions:

1) Line a slow cooker with a large piece of parchment paper.
2) In a small bowl, blend together the spices.
3) Spray the salmon fillet with cooking spray and rub with cooking spray evenly.
4) In the center of the prepared slow cooker, arrange the lemon slices.
5) Now place the salmon fillet on top of the lemon slices.
6) Pour the broth and lemon juice around the fish.
7) Close the lid of the slow cooker and set on "Low" setting for 2 hours.
8) When the cooking time is close to ending, preheat the oven to 400 ºF.
9) After cooking time is finished, uncover the slow cooker and transfer the salmon with liquid into a baking dish.
10) Bake for approximately 5-8 minutes.
11) Meanwhile, for sauce: in a small-sized pan, add the cream, wine and lemon juice over a medium-high heat and bring to the boil, stirring frequently.
12) Now adjust the heat to low and simmer, covered for about 8 minutes.
13) Uncover the pan and stir in the lemon zest.
14) Now adjust the heat to high and cook for about 2 minutes.
15) Remove the pan of sauce from heat and set aside.
16) Remove the baking dish from the oven and place the salmon fillet onto a cutting board.
17) Cut the salmon into 4 equal-sized fillets and top with sauce.
18) Garnish with parsley and serve.

Sardine in Tomato Gravy

Cook time: 8 hours | Serves: 4 | Per Serving: Calories 331, Carbs 8.5g, Fat 24g, Protein 23.3g

Ingredients:

- Olive oil – 2 tbsp.
- Fresh sardines – 1¼ lb. cubed
- Tomatoes – 3, finely chopped
- Garlic cloves – 2, minced
- Tomato puree – ½ C.
- Salt and ground black pepper, as required

Directions:

1) In the pot of a slow cooker, spread the oil evenly.
2) Place the sardines over the oil and top with all of the remaining ingredients.
3) Close the lid of the slow cooker and set on "Low" setting for 8 hours.
4) After cooking time is finished, uncover the slow cooker and serve hot.

Salmon with Lentils

Cook time: 6 hours | Serves: 4 | Per Serving: Calories 387, Carbs 30.6g, Fat 12.7g, Protein 38.3g

Ingredients:

- Lentils – ¾ C. rinsed
- Carrots – ½ C. peeled and finely chopped
- Celery – ¼ C. finely chopped
- Red onion – ¼ C. finely chopped
- Bay leaf – 1
- Low-sodium chicken broth – 2¼ C.
- Olive oil – 1 tbsp.
- Salt and ground black pepper, as required
- Raw honey – 1 tbsp.
- Fresh orange juice – 3-4 tbsp.
- Fresh lemon juice 2 tbsp. divided
- Orange zest – 1 tbsp. grated
- Lemon zest – 1 tsp. grated
- Salmon fillets – 4 (5-oz.)
- Fresh parsley – 2 tbsp. chopped

Directions:

1) In the pot of a slow cooker, add the lentils, carrots, celery, onion, bay leaf and broth and mix well.
2) Arrange a piece of foil onto a smooth surface.
3) Close the lid of the slow cooker and set on "Low" setting for 5-5½ hours.
4) Meanwhile, for glaze: in a small pan set, add the honey, juices and zest over a medium heat and bring to a boil.
5) Adjust the heat to medium and simmer for about 1-2 minutes, stirring continuously.
6) After cooking time is finished, uncover the slow cooker.
7) Place 1 parchment paper over the lentil mixture in slow cooker.
8) Season salmon fillets with salt and black pepper and brush the tops with glaze.
9) Arrange the salmon fillets over the parchment, skin side down.
10) Close the lid of slow cooker and set on "Low" setting for 25-30 minutes.
11) After cooking time is finished, uncover the slow cooker and transfer the salmon fillets onto a platter.
12) Discard the bay leaf and stir the parsley, salt and black pepper into lentil mixture.
13) Serve lentils with salmon fillets.

Parmesan Tilapia

Cook time: 3 hours | Serves: 4 | Per Serving: Calories 188, Carbs 3g, Fat 8.4g, Protein 25.3g

Ingredients:

- Parmesan cheese – ½ C. grated
- Mayonnaise – ¼ C.
- Fresh lemon juice – 2 tbsp.
- Salt and ground black pepper, as required
- Tilapia fillets – 4 (4-oz.)
- Fresh cilantro – 1 tbsp. chopped

Directions:

1) In a bowl, blend together all ingredients except for tilapia fillets and cilantro.
2) Coat the fillets with the mayonnaise mixture evenly.
3) Place the filets over a large piece of foil.
4) Wrap the foil around fillets to seal them.
5) Arrange the foil packet in the pot of a slow cooker.
6) Close the lid of the slow cooker and set on "Low" setting for 3-4 hours.
7) After cooking time is finished, uncover the slow cooker and transfer the foil parcel onto a platter.
8) Carefully open the parcel and serve hot with the garnishing of cilantro.

Haddock with Bell Peppers

Cook time: 4 hours | Serves: 4 | Per Serving: Calories 166, Carbs 8.5g, Fat 3.1g, Protein 25.8g

Ingredients:

- Diced tomatoes – 1 (15-oz.) can
- Bell pepper – 1, seeded and chopped
- Small onion – 1, chopped
- Garlic clove – 1, minced
- Haddock fillets – 1 lb.
- Dried herbs 1 tsp.
- Salt and ground black pepper, as required
- Low-sodium chicken broth – 1/3 C.

Directions:

1) Grease the pot of a slow cooker.
2) In the pot of the slow cooker, place the tomatoes, bell pepper, onion and garlic and stir to combine.
3) Place the fish fillets on top of the tomato mixture and sprinkle with the herbs, salt and black pepper.
4) Place the broth on top evenly.
5) Close the lid of the slow cooker and set on "High" setting for 3-4 hours.

6) After cooking time is finished, uncover the slow cooker and serve hot.

Cheesy Snapper

Cook time: 1 hour 40 minutes | Serves: 4 | Per Serving: Calories 486, Carbs 2.2g, Fat 25.4g, Protein 57.4g

Ingredients:

- Unsalted butter – 4 tbsp.
- Almond flour – 2 tbsp.
- Dry mustard – ½ tbsp.
- Ground nutmeg – ¼ tbsp.
- Salt, as required
- Unsweetened almond milk – 1 C.
- Fresh lemon juice – 1 tsp.
- Cheddar cheese – ¾ C. shredded
- Frozen snapper fillets – 4 (7-oz.) thawed

Directions:

1) In a medium-sized saucepan, melt butter over medium heat and cook flour, mustard, nutmeg and salt for about 2 minutes, stirring continuously.
2) Slowly add the milk, stirring continuously until smooth.
3) Stir in the lemon juice and cheese and cook until cheese is melted, stirring continuously.
4) Remove the pan of cheese sauce from the heat.
5) In the pot of a slow cooker, place the fish fillets and top with cheese sauce evenly.
6) Close the lid of the slow cooker and set on "High" setting for 1½ hours.
7) After cooking time is finished, uncover the slow cooker and serve hot.

Cod with Olives

Cook time: 2 hours | Serves: 4 | Per Serving: Calories 130, Carbs 6.8g, Fat 2.2g, Protein 21.8g

Ingredients:

- Cod fillets – 1 lb.
- Small onion – 1, chopped
- Garlic cloves – 2, minced
- Dried dill – 1 tsp.
- Cayenne pepper – ¼ tsp.
- Salt and ground black pepper, as required
- Low-sodium chicken broth – ½ C.
- Large tomatoes – 2, chopped
- Olives – ¼ C. pitted and sliced

Directions:

1) In the bottom of a slow cooker, place the cod fillets.
2) Place onion and garlic over cod.

3) Sprinkle with dill, cayenne pepper, salt and black pepper.
4) Pour broth on top.
5) Close the lid of the slow cooker and set on "Low" setting for 1½ hours.
6) After cooking time is finished, uncover the slow cooker and stir in tomatoes and olives.
7) Again close the lid of the slow cooker and set on "Low" setting for 30 minutes.
8) After cooking time is finished, uncover the slow cooker and serve.

Seafood Gumbo

Cook time: 5 hours 20 minutes | Serves: 4 | Per Serving: Calories 455, Carbs 17.8g, Fat 19.3g, Protein 47.8g

Ingredients:

- Bacon slices – 1/3 lb. chopped
- Bell pepper – 1, seeded and chopped
- Medium onion – 1, chopped
- Celery stalk – 1, chopped
- Garlic cloves – 2, minced
- Diced tomatoes – 1 (14-oz.) can
- Low-sodium chicken broth – 2 C.
- Dried rosemary – 1 tsp. crushed
- Frozen okra – 8 oz. thawed and cut into ½-inch pieces
- Fresh crabmeat – ¾ lb.
- Shrimp – ¾ lb. peeled and deveined
- Scallion (green part) – 2 tbsp. chopped

Directions:

1) Heat a large-sized non-stick wok over a medium heat and cook the bacon for about 8-10 minutes or until crisp.
2) With a slotted spoon, transfer the bacon into the pot of a slow cooker.
3) Drain most of the fats from the wok.
4) In the same wok with bacon fat, add bell pepper, celery, onion and garlic and cook for about 8-10 minutes.
5) Transfer the vegetable mixture into the slow cooker.
6) Add remaining ingredients except for okra and seafood and stir to combine.
7) Close the lid of the slow cooker and set on "Low" setting for 4 hours.
8) After cooking time is finished, uncover the slow cooker and stir in the remaining ingredients.
9) Again, close the lid of the slow cooker and set on "High" setting for 1 hour.
10) After cooking time is finished, uncover the slow cooker and serve hot.

Shrimp & Cauliflower Curry

Cook time: 2 hours | Serves: 4 | Per Serving: Calories 268, Carbs 12.3g, Fat 10.9g, Protein 28.4g

Ingredients:

- Tomatoes – 2 C. finely chopped
- Small cauliflower florets – 1 C.
- Celery stalk – 1, chopped
- Small yellow onion – 1, chopped
- Unsweetened coconut milk – 1 C.
- Curry powder – 2 tbsp.
- Salt and ground black pepper, as required
- Shrimp – 1 lb. peeled and deveined

Directions:

1) In the pot of a slow cooker, add all ingredients except for shrimp and stir to combine.
2) Close the lid of the slow cooker and set on "High" setting for 80 minutes.
3) After cooking time is finished, uncover the slow cooker and stir in the shrimp.
4) Again, close the lid of the slow cooker and set on "High" setting for 40 minutes.
5) After cooking time is finished, uncover the slow cooker and serve hot.

Wine Braised Shrimp & Veggies

Cook time: 5 hours | Serves: 4 | Per Serving: Calories 244, Carbs 18.6g, Fat 3.3g, Protein 29.8g

Ingredients:

- Medium onion – 1, chopped
- Medium bell pepper – ½, seeded and chopped
- Whole tomatoes with juices – 1 (14½-oz.) can, chopped roughly
- Sliced mushrooms – 1 (2½-oz.) jar
- Ripe olives – ¼ C. pitted and sliced
- Garlic cloves – 2, minced
- Low-sodium chicken broth – 1 (14½-oz.) can
- Tomato sauce – 1 (8-oz.) can
- Dry white wine – ½ C.
- Fresh orange juice – ½ C.
- Dried basil – 1 tsp.
- Bay leaves – 2
- Salt and ground black pepper, as required
- Medium shrimp – 1 lb. peeled

Directions:

1) In the pot of a slow cooker, place all the ingredients except for shrimp and stir to combine.
2) Close the lid of the slow cooker and set on "Low" setting for 4-4½ hours.
3) After cooking time is finished, uncover the slow cooker and stir in the shrimp.
4) Again, close the lid of the slow cooker and set on "Low" setting for 20-30 minutes.
5) After cooking time is finished, uncover the slow cooker and discard the bay leaves
6) Serve hot.

Vegetarian & Vegan Recipes

Broccoli in Cheesy Tomato Sauce

Cook time: 6 hours | Serves: 4 | Per Serving: Calories 133, Carbs 12.6g, Fat 6.2g, Protein 9.1g

Ingredients:

- Broccoli florets – 4 C.
- Small onion – 1, chopped
- Fresh rosemary – 1 tbsp. minced
- Swiss cheese – ¾ C. torn
- tomato sauce – 1 C.
- Fresh lemon juice – ½ tbsp.
- Salt and ground black pepper, as required

Directions:

1) In the pot of a slow cooker, place all ingredients and mix well.
2) Close the lid of the slow cooker and set on "Low" setting for 6-7 hours.
3) After cooking time is finished, uncover the slow cooker and serve hot.

Creamy Mushrooms

Cook time: 4 hours | Serves: 4 | Per Serving: Calories 59, Carbs 9.2g, Fat 1.3g, Protein 5.7g

Ingredients:

- Fresh mushrooms – 1¼ lb. halved
- Onion – 1, sliced thinly
- Garlic cloves – 3, minced
- Smoked paprika – 2 tsp.
- Low-sodium vegetable broth – 1 C.
- Sour cream – 1 tbsp.
- Salt and ground black pepper, as required
- Fresh parsley – 4 tbsp. chopped

Directions:

1) In the pot of a slow cooker, place the mushrooms, onion, garlic, paprika and broth and stir to combine.
2) Close the lid of the slow cooker and set on "High" setting for 4 hours.
3) After cooking time is finished, uncover the slow cooker and stir in the sour cream, salt and black pepper.
4) Serve with a garnishing of parsley.

Mushrooms with Pearl Onions

Cook time: 8 hours | Serves: 4 | Per Serving: Calories 50, Carbs 8.8g, Fat 0.4g, Protein 4.7g

Ingredients:

- Fresh medium mushrooms – 1 lb.
- Frozen pearl onions – 7 oz. thawed
- Low-sodium vegetable broth – 1¼ C.
- Balsamic vinegar – 2 tbsp.
- Salt, as required

Directions:

1) In the pot of a slow cooker, place all the ingredients and mix well.
2) Close the lid of the slow cooker and set on "Low" setting for 6-8 hours.
3) After cooking time is finished, uncover the slow cooker and serve hot.

Mushroom Casserole

Cook time: 6 hours | Serves: 4 | Per Serving: Calories 174, Carbs 3.6g, Fat 11.8g, Protein 14.2g

Ingredients:

- Eggs – 8
- Unsweetened almond milk – 1/3 C.
- Salt and ground black pepper, as required
- Fresh mushrooms – 2 C. sliced
- Sun-dried tomatoes – 1/3 C.
- Onion – 1 tbsp. chopped
- Garlic – 1 tsp. minced
- Feta cheese – 1/3 C. crumbled

Directions:

1) In a large-sized bowl, add the eggs, almond milk, salt and black and beat well blended.
2) Add the remaining ingredients except for cheese and stir to combine.
3) In the bottom of a greased Slow Cooker, place the egg mixture and top with the cheese.
4) Close the lid of the slow cooker and set on "Low" setting for 4-6 hours.
5) After cooking time is finished, uncover the slow cooker and
6) Cut into equal-sized wedges and serve hot.

Cauliflower Casserole

Cook time: 5 hours | Serves: 4 | Per Serving: Calories 279, Carbs 11.2g, Fat 20.7g, Protein 14.8g

Ingredients:

- Frozen cauliflower – 24 oz.
- Cream cheese – 4 oz. cubed
- Mozzarella cheese – 1 C. shredded
- Cheddar cheese – 1 C. shredded
- Scallions – 2, chopped

Directions:

1) Grease the pot of a slow cooker generously.
2) In the prepared pot, place half of the cauliflower in an even layer.
3) Place half of cream cheese cubes over cauliflower, followed by half of both cheeses.
4) Repeat the layers once.
5) Close the lid of the slow cooker and set on "Low" setting for 4-5 hours.
6) After cooking time is finished, uncover the slow cooker and serve hot with the garnishing of scallion.

Ratatouille

Cook time: 6 hours | Serves: 4 | Per Serving: Calories 157, Carbs 14.8g, Fat 11.1g, Protein 3.3g

Ingredients:

- Fresh basil – ½ C.
- Garlic cloves – 2, minced
- Olive oil – 3 tbsp.
- White wine vinegar – 1 tbsp.
- Fresh lemon juice – 1 tbsp.
- Tomato paste – 1 tbsp.
- Salt, as required
- Medium zucchini – 1, cut into small chunks
- Medium summer squash – 1, cut into small chunks
- Medium eggplant – 1, cut into small chunks
- Small white onion – 1, cut into small chunks
- Cherry tomatoes – 1 C.

Directions:

1) In a clean food processor, add basil, garlic, oil, vinegar, lemon juice, tomato paste and salt, and pulse until smooth.
2) In the pot of a slow cooker, place all the vegetables and top with the pureed mixture evenly.
3) Close the lid of the slow cooker and set on "Low" setting for 5-6 hours.
4) After cooking time is finished, uncover the slow cooker and serve hot.

Veggies in Curry Sauce

Cook time: 6 hours | Serves: 4 | Per Serving: Calories 318, Carbs 28.2g, Fat 19.4g, Protein 7.2g

Ingredients:

For Curry Sauce:

- Low-sodium vegetable broth – 2 C.
- Unsweetened coconut milk – 2 C (this is added towards the end of the cook)
- Yellow curry powder – 2 tbsp.
- Ground cumin – 1 tsp.
- Cayenne pepper – ½ tsp.

For Veggies:

- Small cauliflower head – 1, trimmed leaves and stems
- Small red potatoes – 2, quartered
- Bell pepper – 1, seeded and sliced thinly
- Onion – ½, chopped
- Garlic cloves – 2, sliced
- Cashews – 2 tbsp. toasted

Directions:

1) For curry sauce: in a large-sized bowl, add all ingredients except the coconut milk; and beat until well blended.
2) In the pot of a slow cooker, place the whole cauliflower, potatoes, bell peppers, onion and garlic.
3) Pour curry sauce on top and stir well.
4) Close the lid of slow cooker and set on "High" setting for 2-3 hours.
5) In the last 10-15 minutes of cooking, stir in coconut milk.
6) After cooking time is finished, uncover the slow cooker and cut the cauliflower head into wedges.
7) Divide cauliflower into bowls and top with the curry sauce and cashews.
8) Serve immediately.

Three Veggies Curry

Cook time: 4½ hours | Serves: 4 | Per Serving: Calories 288, Carbs 47.8g, Fat 8g, Protein 9.3g

Ingredients:

- Olive oil – 2 tbsp.
- Medium onion – 1, chopped
- Medium potatoes – 4, peeled and chopped
- Medium cauliflower head – 1, broken into florets
- Garlic cloves – 2, sliced
- Tomato paste – 2 tbsp.
- Low-sodium vegetable broth – 1¼ C.
- Garam masala powder – 1 tsp.
- Ground cumin – ½ tsp.
- Ginger powder – ½ tsp.
- Salt and ground black pepper, as required
- Frozen peas – 1 C.

Directions:

1) In the pot of a slow cooker, add all ingredients except for peas and stir to blend.
2) Close the lid of the slow cooker and set on "High" setting for 4 hours.
3) After cooking time is finished, uncover the slow cooker and stir in peas.
4) Again, close the lid of the slow cooker and set on "High" setting for 30 minutes.
5) After cooking time is finished, uncover the slow cooker and serve hot.

Mixed Veggie Curry

Cook time: 4½ hours | Serves: 4 | Per Serving: Calories 387, Carbs 46g, Fat 19.5g, Protein 8.2g

Ingredients:

- Russet potatoes 3, peeled and cut into 1-inch cubes
- Carrot – 1 C. peeled and sliced
- Bell pepper – 1, seeded and chopped
- Curry powder – 2 tbsp.
- Whole-wheat flour – 2 tbsp.
- Red chili powder – 1 tbsp.
- Coconut cream – 12 oz.
- Green peas – 1 C. shelled
- Fresh cilantro – 2 tbsp. chopped

Directions:

1) In the pot of a slow cooker, add all ingredients except for peas and cilantro and stir to combine.
2) Close the lid of the slow cooker and set on "High" setting for 3-4 hours.
3) After cooking time is finished, uncover the slow cooker and stir in peas.
4) Again, close the lid of the slow cooker and set on "High" setting for 30 minutes.
5) After cooking time is finished, uncover the slow cooker and serve hot with the garnishing of cilantro.

Veggie Casserole

Cook time: 4½ hours | Serves: 4 | Per Serving: Calories 128, Carbs 10.3g, Fat 7.3g, Protein 8.2g

Ingredients:

- Unsalted butter – 1 tbsp. melted
- Medium zucchinis – 2, peeled and cut in rounds
- Small bell pepper – 1, seeded and cut into strips
- Fresh tomatoes – 1 C. finely chopped
- Small white onion – 1, sliced thinly
- Fresh thyme – 1 tbsp. minced
- Parmesan cheese – ¼ C. grated
- Salt and ground black pepper, as required

Directions:

1) In the pot of a slow cooker, place all ingredients except for cheese and mix well.
2) Close the lid of the slow cooker and set on "Low" setting for 3 hours.
3) After cooking time is finished, uncover the slow cooker and sprinkle with cheese evenly.
4) Close the lid of the slow cooker and set on "Low" setting for 1½ hours.
5) After cooking time is finished, uncover the slow cooker and serve hot.

Stuffed Bell Peppers

Cook time: 4¼ hours | Serves: 4 | Per Serving: Calories 444, Carbs 65g, Fat 1g, Protein 26.2g

Ingredients:

- Large bell peppers – 4
- Olive oil – 1 tbsp.
- Onion – 1 C. chopped
- Garlic – 1 tbsp. minced
- Low-fat cheddar cheese – 1½ C. divided
- Cooked quinoa – 1 C.
- Black beans – 1 (15-oz.) can, rinsed and drained
- Tomato salsa – 1 C.
- Fresh parsley – 2 tbsp. minced
- Ground cumin – ½ tsp.
- Cayenne pepper – ½ tsp.

Directions:

1) Remove the stem of each bell pepper.
2) Cut about ½-inch off tops of each bell pepper and then chop them.
3) Remove the seeds from inside to create a cup.

4) In a non-stick wok, heat oil over a medium heat and sauté onion, garlic and chopped bell pepper tops for about 4-5 minutes.
5) Transfer the onion mixture into a large-sized bowl.
6) Add 1 C. Of cheese and remaining ingredients and stir to combine.
7) Stuff the bell peppers with cheese mixture.
8) In the pot of a slow cooker, add 1/3 C. Of water.
9) Arrange bell peppers in the pot of slow cooker.
10) Close the lid of the slow cooker and set on "High" setting for 3-4 hours.
11) After cooking time is finished, uncover the slow cooker and top each bell pepper with remaining cheese evenly.
12) Close the lid of the slow cooker and set on "High" setting for 10 minutes.
13) After cooking time is finished, uncover the slow cooker and serve hot.

Stuffed Potatoes

Cook time: 8 hours | Serves: 4 | Per Serving: Calories 275, Carbs 43g, Fat 8.1g, Protein 10.2g

Ingredients:

- Medium – 4 russet potatoes
- Broccoli head – 1
- Olive oil – 2 tbsp.
- Fresh cremini mushrooms – 10 oz. trimmed and quartered
- Salt and ground black pepper, as required
- Low-sodium vegetable broth – ¼-½ C.
- low-fat plain Greek yogurt – 2/3 C.

Directions:

1) Wrap each potato in a piece of foil and place in the pot of a slow cooker.
2) Close the lid of the slow cooker and set on "Low" setting for 8 hours.
3) Meanwhile, cut the broccoli head into small florets.
4) Peel stalks and cut into ½-inch pieces
5) In a large-sized wok, heat oil over a medium-high heat and cook mushrooms for about 2 minutes.
6) Add broccoli, salt and black pepper and cook for about 8 minutes, stirring frequently.
7) After cooking time is finished, uncover the slow cooker and transfer the potatoes onto a plate.
8) Remove the foil and cut each potato in half lengthwise.
9) Carefully, scoop out flesh and transfer into a bowl, reserving skins.
10) In the bowl of potato flesh, add broth, yogurt and black pepper and stir well blended.
11) Divide potato flesh mixture into potato skins evenly and top with broccoli mixture.
12) Serve immediately.

Beans Curry

Cook time: 10 hours 6 minutes | Serves: 4 | Per Serving: Calories 419, Carbs 72.5g, Fat 5.5g, Protein 24.1g

Ingredients:

- Canola oil – 1 tbsp.
- Medium white onion – 1, chopped
- Fresh ginger – 1 tbsp. minced
- Garlic – 1 tsp. minced
- Curry powder – 2 tsp.
- Ground cumin – ½ tsp.
- Red pepper flakes – ¼ tsp. crushed
- Tomato paste – 6 oz.
- Fat-free plain Greek yogurt – 8 oz.
- Water – ½ C.
- Red kidney beans – 2 (15-oz.) cans rinsed and drained

Directions:

1) In a large-sized wok, heat oil over a medium heat and sauté onion for about 4-5 minutes.
2) Add ginger, garlic, curry powder and spices and sauté for about 1 minute.
3) Stir in tomato paste, yogurt and water and immediately remove from heat.
4) Meanwhile, place beans in the pot of a slow cooker.
5) Pour the yogurt mixture over beans and gently stir to combine.
6) Close the lid of the slow cooker and set on "Low" setting for 8-10 hours.
7) After cooking time is finished, uncover the slow cooker and serve hot.

Beans with Veggies & Feta

Cook time: 4 hours | Serves: 4 | Per Serving: Calories 205, Carbs 32.6g, Fat 4.2g, Protein 11.6g

Ingredients:

- Cannellini beans – 1½ (15-oz.) cans, rinsed and drained
- Diced tomatoes with basil, garlic and oregano – 1 (14-oz.) can
- Zucchini – ¾ C. chopped
- Bell pepper – ¾ C. seeded and chopped
- Kalamata olives – 1/3 C. pitted and halved
- Fresh parsley – 2 tbsp. chopped
- Ground black pepper, as required
- Fresh lemon juice – 2 tbsp.
- Low-sodium vegetable broth – ¾ C.
- Feta cheese – ¼ C. Crumbled
- Garlic cloves – 2, minced

Directions:

1) In the pot of a slow cooker, place all the ingredients except for cheese and stir to combine.
2) Close the lid of the slow cooker and set on "High" setting for 4 hours.
3) After cooking time is finished, uncover the slow cooker and serve hot with the topping of feta cheese.

Chickpeas with Veggies

Cook time: 5 hours | Serves: 4 | Per Serving: Calories 228, Carbs 40.7g, Fat 5.7g, Protein 8.8g

Ingredients:

- Olive oil – 1 tbsp.
- Onion – 1, sliced thinly
- Garlic cloves – 2, minced
- Canned chickpeas – 20 oz. rinsed and drained
- Zucchini – 1 C. chopped
- Roasted red peppers – 1 C. chopped
- Olives – ½ C. pitted
- Low-sodium vegetable broth – ¾ C.
- Capers – 1 tbsp.
- Dried rosemary – 1 tsp.
- Dried oregano – 1 tsp.
- Bay leaf – 1
- Salt and ground black pepper, as required

Directions:

1) In a small-sized wok, heat the oil over a medium-high heat and sauté the onions and garlic for about 4-5 minutes.
2) Transfer the onion into the slow cooker with the remaining ingredients and stir to combine.
3) Close the lid of the slow cooker and set on "Low" setting for 5 hours.
4) After cooking time is finished, uncover the slow cooker and serve hot.

Chickpeas with Quinoa

Cook time: 4½ hours | Serves: 4 | Per Serving: Calories 360, Carbs 54.1g, Fat 10.9g, Protein 12.8g

Ingredients:

- Low-sodium vegetable broth – 2 C.
- Uncooked quinoa – 1 C. rinsed
- Chickpeas – 1 (14-oz.) can, drained and rinsed
- Red onions – ¾ C. sliced
- Garlic cloves – 2, minced
- Olive oil – 2 tbsp.
- Salt, as required
- Fresh lemon juice – 2 tsp.
- Roasted red bell peppers – 1/3 C. drained and chopped
- Fresh arugula – 3 C.

Directions:

1) In the pot of a slow cooker, place the broth, quinoa, chickpeas, onions, garlic, 1½ tsp. of the oil and salt and stir to combine.
2) Close the lid of slow cooker and set on "Low" setting for 3-4 hours.
3) Meanwhile, in a bowl, add the lemon juice, remaining oil and some salt and mix well.
4) After cooking time is finished, uncover the slow cooker and with a fork, fluff the quinoa mixture.
5) After cooking time is finished, uncover the slow cooker and stir in the olive oil mixture, bell peppers and arugula.
6) Close the lid of the slow cooker and set on "High" setting for 30 minutes.
7) After cooking time is finished, uncover the slow cooker and serve hot.

Chickpeas & Veggie Curry

Cook time: 6 hours 20 minutes | Serves: 4 | Per Serving: Calories 278, Carbs 51.2g, Fat 5.1g, Protein 10.2g

Ingredients:

- Olive oil – 1 tbsp.
- Onion – 1 C. chopped
- Carrot – ½ C. peeled and cut into ¼-inch thick slices
- Garlic cloves – 2, minced
- Fresh ginger – 1 tsp. grated
- Serrano pepper – 1, seeded and minced
- Curry powder – 1 tbsp.
- Cooked chickpeas – 2 C.
- Baking potatoes – 1 C. peeled and cubed
- Fresh green beans – ¾ C. trimmed and cut into 1-inch pieces
- Green bell pepper – ½ C. seeded and chopped
- Diced tomatoes with juices – 1 (14½-oz.) can
- Red chili powder – ¼ tsp.
- Salt and ground black pepper, as required
- Low-sodium vegetable broth – 12 oz.
- Fresh baby spinach – 2 C.
- Light coconut milk – 1 C.

Directions:

1) In a large non-stick wok, heat oil over a medium heat and cook onion and carrot for about 3-4 minutes.
2) Add garlic, ginger, Serrano pepper and curry powder and sauté for about 1 minute.
3) Transfer onion mixture into a slow cooker.

4) Stir in chickpeas, potatoes, green beans, bell pepper, tomatoes with juices, red chili powder, salt, black pepper and broth.
5) Close the lid of the slow cooker and set on "High" setting for 6 hours.
6) After cooking time is finished, uncover the slow cooker and stir in spinach and coconut milk.
7) Close the lid of the slow cooker and set on "High" setting for 15 minutes.
8) After cooking time is finished, uncover the slow cooker and and serve immediately.

Spicy Lentils

Cook time: 6 hours | Serves: 4 | Per Serving: Calories 299, Carbs 51.8g, Fat 1.7g, Protein 20.4g

Ingredients:

- Split red lentils – 1½ C. rinsed
- Water – 4 C.
- Diced tomatoes – 1 (14-oz.) can
- Medium onion – 1, diced
- Fresh ginger – 1 (1-inch) piece, grated finely
- cumin seeds – 2 tsp. toasted
- mustard seeds – 1 tsp. toasted
- fennel seeds – 1 tsp. toasted
- Ground turmeric – 1 tsp.
- Salt and ground black pepper, as required
- Fresh cilantro leaves – 2 tbsp. chopped

Directions:

1) In the pot of a slow cooker, add all ingredients except for cilantro and stir to combine.
2) Close the lid of the slow cooker and set on "Low" setting for 4-6 hours.
3) After cooking time is finished, uncover the slow cooker and stir in lemon juice.
4) Serve hot with a garnishing of cilantro.

Macaroni & Chickpea Casserole

Cook time: 6 hours | Serves: 4 | Per Serving: Calories 369, Carbs 68.3g, Fat 5g, Protein 16.9g

Ingredients:

- Chickpeas – 1 (15-oz.) can, rinsed and drained
- Medium carrots – 3, peeled and sliced
- Medium onion – 1, chopped
- Diced tomatoes with juices – 1 (28-oz.) can
- Garlic cloves – 2, finely chopped
- Tomato paste – 1 (6-oz.) can
- Water – 1 C.
- Coconut sugar – 2 tsp.
- Italian seasoning – 1 tsp.
- Salt and ground black pepper, as required
- Frozen cut green beans – 1½ C. thawed
- Uncooked elbow macaroni – 1 C.
- Parmesan cheese – ½ C. shredded

Directions:

1) In the pot of a slow cooker, place all the ingredients except for green beans, macaroni and parmesan cheese and stir to combine.
2) Close the lid of the slow cooker and set on "Low" setting for 6-8 hours.
3) After cooking time is finished, uncover the slow cooker and stir in the green beans and macaroni.
4) Close the lid of the slow cooker and set on "High" setting for 20-30 minutes.
5) After cooking time is finished, uncover the slow cooker and serve hot with the topping of cheese.

Spinach Risotto

Cook time: 5 hours │Serves: 4 │ Per Serving: Calories 184, Carbs 28.1g, Fat 5.5g, Protein 5.3g

Ingredients:

- Uncooked brown rice – ¾ C.
- Fresh mushrooms – ½ C. sliced
- Water – 1¾ C.
- Garlic powder – ½ tsp.
- Ground black pepper, as required
- Fresh spinach – 1 C. torn
- Fresh basil leaves – 2 tbsp. chopped
- Fresh lemon peel – 1 tsp. grated finely
- Olive oil – 1 tbsp.
- Parmesan cheese – 3-4tbsp. grated freshly

Directions:

1) In the pot of a slow cooker, add rice, mushrooms, water, garlic powder and black pepper and stir to combine.
2) Close the lid of the slow cooker and set on "Low" setting for 4-4½ hours.
3) After cooking time is finished, uncover the slow cooker and stir in remaining ingredients except for cheese.
4) Close the lid of the slow cooker and set on "Low" setting 30 minutes.
5) After cooking time is finished, uncover the slow cooker and stir in Parmesan until melted.
6) Serve hot.

Side Dish Recipes

Cauliflower Mash

Cook time: 3 hours | Serves: 4 | Per Serving: Calories 130, Carbs 8.5g, Fat 8.9g, Protein 4.8g

Ingredients:

- Cauliflower head – 1, cut into bite-sized pieces
- Garlic cloves – 4, smashed
- Low-sodium vegetable broth – 4 C.
- Fat-free plain Greek yogurt – 1/3 C.
- Unsalted butter – 3 tbsp. cut into cubes
- Fresh chives – 1 tbsp. chopped
- Fresh parsley – 1 tbsp. chopped
- Fresh rosemary – 1 tbsp. chopped
- Salt and ground black pepper, as required

Directions:

1) In the pot of a slow cooker, place the cauliflower, garlic and broth and stir to combine.
2) Close the lid of slow cooker and set on "High" setting for 2½-3 hours.
3) After cooking time is finished, uncover the slow cooker and through a strainer, drain the cauliflower and garlic, reserving ½ C. of the broth.
4) Transfer the cauliflower into a bowl and with a potato masher, mash the cauliflower slightly.
5) Add the yogurt, butter and desired amount of reserved broth and mash until smooth.
6) Add the herbs, salt and black pepper and stir to combine.
7) Serve warm.

Mashed Potatoes

Cook time: 2½ hours | Serves: 4 | Per Serving: Calories 184, Carbs 27.1g, Fat 7g, Protein 4.4g

Ingredients:

- Medium red potatoes – 3, cut into ½-inch thick slices
- Scallions – ¼ C. chopped
- Fresh oregano – ½ tbsp. chopped
- Extra-virgin olive oil – 1 tbsp.
- Fresh lemon juice – 1 tbsp.
- Feta cheese – 1 oz. crumbled
- Half-and-half – ¼ C.
- Fresh parsley – 2 tbsp. chopped

Directions:

1) In the pot of a slow cooker, place the potatoes, scallions, oregano oil and lemon juice and mix well.
2) Close the lid of the slow cooker and set on "High" setting for 2½ hours.
3) After cooking time is finished, uncover the slow cooker and stir in the feta cheese and half-and-half.
4) With a potato masher, mash the potato mixture until smooth and creamy.
5) Serve warm with the garnishing of parsley.

Cheesy Spinach

Cook time: 1 hour │ Serves: 4 │ Per Serving: Calories 214, Carbs 5.1g, Fat 17.2g, Protein 11.9g

Ingredients:

- Low-fat cream cheese – 3 oz. softened
- Fresh baby spinach – 16 oz.
- Cheddar cheese – 1 C. shredded
- Salt and ground black pepper, as required

Directions:

1) In the pot of a slow cooker, place the cream cheese and top with spinach, followed by cheddar cheese.
2) Close the lid of the slow cooker and set on "High" setting for 1 hour
3) After cooking time is finished, uncover the slow cooker and stir in salt and black pepper.
4) Serve hot.

Buttered Collard Greens

Cook time: 6 hours │ Serves: 4 │ Per Serving: Calories 77, Carbs 4.4g, Fat 6.2g, Protein 2.6g

Ingredients:

- Unsalted butter – 2 tbsp. melted
- Collard greens – 6 C. rinsed
- Salt and ground black pepper, as required
- Low-sodium vegetable broth – 2 C.
- Fresh lime juice – 1 tbsp.

Directions:

1) Remove any thick stems of greens and then chop leaves into strips
2) In the pot of a slow cooker, spread the butter
3) Add the greens, salt, pepper, and broth and stir to combine.
4) Close the lid of slow cooker and set on "Low" setting for 6 hours.
5) After cooking time is finished, uncover the slow cooker and drizzle with lemon juice.
6) Serve hot.

Lemony Kale

Cook time: 4 hours 10 minutes | Serves: 4 | Per Serving: Calories 191, Carbs 16.6g, Fat 9.5g, Protein 7.6g

Ingredients:

- Olive oil – 1 tbsp.
- Small onion – 1, chopped
- Garlic cloves – 2, minced
- Red pepper flakes – ½ tsp. crushed
- Fresh kale – 1½ lb. Tough ribs removed and chopped
- Low-sodium vegetable broth – 1½-2 C.
- Fresh lemon juice – 2 tbsp.
- Salt and ground black pepper, as required
- Pine nuts – 4 tbsp.

Directions:

1) In a large-sized non-stick wok, heat oil over medium heat and sauté onion for about 5-6 minutes.
2) Add garlic and red pepper flakes and sauté for 1 minute more.
3) Add kale and cook for 2-3 minutes.
4) Transfer the kale mixture into the pot of a slow cooker.
5) Add remaining ingredients and mix.
6) Close the lid of the slow cooker and set on "Low" setting for 3½-4 hours.
7) After cooking time is finished, uncover the slow cooker and immediately stir in pine nuts.
8) Serve hot.

Garlicky Mushrooms

Cook time: 3 hours | Serves: 4 | Per Serving: Calories 118, Carbs 6.7g, Fat 9.2g, Protein 5.7g

Ingredients:

- Fresh button mushrooms – 1½ lb. quartered
- Garlic cloves – 3, minced
- Fresh parsley – ¼ C. chopped
- Salt and ground black pepper, as required
- Unsalted butter – 3 tbsp. melted
- Fresh lemon zest – 1 tsp. grated finely

Directions:

1) In the pot of a slow cooker, add all ingredients except for lemon zest and mix well.
2) Close the lid of the slow cooker and set on "High" setting for 3 hours.
3) After cooking time is finished, uncover the slow cooker and serve with the topping of lemon zest.

Balsamic Brussels Sprouts

Cook time: 4 hours │Serves: 4 │ Per Serving: Calories 210, Carbs 27.8g, Fat 10.5g, Protein 5.8g

Ingredients:

- Balsamic vinegar – 1/3 C.
- Brown sugar – 1½ tbsp.
- Brussels sprouts – 1½ lb. trimmed and halved
- Olive oil – 2 tbsp.
- Salt and ground black pepper, as required
- Unsalted butter – 1 tbsp. cubed

Directions:

1) In the pot of a slow cooker, place the Brussels sprouts, olive oil, salt and black pepper, and stir to combine.
2) Place the butter cubes on top.
3) Close the lid of the slow cooker and set on "Low" setting for 3-4 hours.
4) Meanwhile, for balsamic reduction: in a small-sized pan, add the vinegar and brown sugar over medium heat and bring to a gentle boil.
5) Cook for about 6-8 minutes, stirring frequently.
6) Remove the pan of reduction from the heat and set aside to cool.
7) After cooking time is finished, uncover the slow cooker and transfer the Brussels sprouts into a bowl.
8) Drizzle with balsamic reduction and serve immediately.

Garlicky Green Beans

Cook time: 8 hours │Serves: 4 │ Per Serving: Calories 53, Carbs 11.4g, Fat 0.2g, Protein 3.3g

Ingredients:

- Fresh green beans – 1½ lb. trimmed
- Yellow onion – ½, finely chopped
- Garlic cloves – 2, minced
- Salt and ground black pepper, as required
- Low-sodium vegetable broth – 1½ C.

Directions:

1) In the pot of a slow cooker, place all ingredients and stir to combine.
2) Close the lid of the slow cooker and set on "Low" setting for 6-8 hours.
3) After cooking time is finished, uncover the slow cooker and serve.

Baked Beans

Cook time: 4 hours 12 minutes |Serves: 4 | Per Serving: Calories 422, Carbs 58.4g, Fat 12.6g, Protein 21.9g

Ingredients:

- Uncooked bacon – 4 oz. chopped
- Small yellow onion – 1, diced
- Garlic cloves – 2, minced
- Canned white beans – 7 oz. rinsed and drained
- Canned pinto beans – 7 oz. rinsed and drained
- Canned kidney beans – 7 oz. rinsed and drained
- Ketchup – 1/3 C.
- Spicy BBQ sauce – 2 tbsp.
- Molasses – 2 tbsp.
- Dark brown sugar – 2-3 tbsp.
- Worcestershire sauce – ½ tbsp.
- Yellow mustard – ¼ tbsp.

Directions:

1) Heat a non-stick wok over a medium-high heat and cook the bacon for about 8-10 minutes, stirring frequently.
2) With a slotted spoon, transfer the bacon onto a paper towel-lined plate to drain.
3) Drain the bacon grease, leaving a little in the wok.
4) In the same wok with bacon grease, add onion and garlic and sauté for about 1-2 minutes.
5) Transfer the onion mixture into the pot of a slow cooker.
6) Add the cooked bacon and remaining ingredients and stir to combine.
7) Close the lid of the slow cooker and set on "High" setting for 3-4 hours.
8) After cooking time is finished, uncover the slow cooker and serve hot.

Simple Rice

Cook time: 2½ hours | Serves: 4 | Per Serving: Calories 185, Carbs 36g, Fat 2.9g, Protein 3g

Ingredients:

- Jasmine rice – 1 C. rinsed
- Unsalted butter – 1 tbsp.
- Pinch of salt
- Water – 1½ C.

Directions:

1) In the pot of a slow cooker, place all ingredients and stir to combine.
2) Close the lid of the slow cooker and set on "Low" setting for 2-2½ hours.
3) After cooking time is finished, uncover the slow cooker and with a fork, fluff the rice.
4) Serve warm.

Dessert Recipes

Chocolate Fondue

Cook time: 1 hour | Serves: 4 | Per Serving: Calories 214, Carbs 25.6g, Fat 11.9g, Protein 1.9g

Ingredients:

- Dark chocolate – 3 oz. chopped
- Heavy cream – ½ C.
- Brewed coffee – ½ oz.
- Sugar – ¼ C.
- Liquid stevia – 1/8 tsp.
- Vanilla extract – ½ tsp.

Directions:

1) Line the pot of a slow cooker with greased parchment paper.
2) In the pot of slow cooker, add all the ingredients and stir to combine.
3) Close the lid of the slow cooker and set on "Low" setting for 1 hour.
4) After cooking time is finished, uncover the slow cooker and with a wire whisk, mix until smooth.
5) Serve warm.

Vanilla Custard

Cook time: 2 hours | Serves: 4 | Per Serving: Calories 171, Carbs 1.9g, Fat 16g, Protein 4.9g

Ingredients:

- Heavy cream – 1 C.
- Unsweetened almond milk – ½ C.
- Erythritol – ¼ C.
- Eggs – 2
- Egg yolks – 2
- Vanilla extract – 1 tsp.
- Ground cinnamon – ½ tsp.
- Salt – ¼ tsp.

Directions:

1) In the bowl of a stand mixer, add all the ingredients and beat using a medium-high speed until blended well.
2) Place the custard mixture into greased 4 ramekins evenly about ¾ of the way full.
3) In the pot of a slow cooker, place a rack and pour 2 C. of hot water.
4) Arrange the ramekins on top of the rack.

5) Close the lid of the slow cooker and set on "High" setting for 2 hours.
6) After cooking time is finished, uncover the slow cooker and place the ramekins onto a wire rack to cool for about 1 hour.
7) Refrigerate for about 2 hours before serving.

Blueberry Custard

Cook time: 3 hours | Serves: 4 | Per Serving: Calories 345, Carbs 15.6g, Fat 26.8g, Protein 11.9g

Ingredients:

- Large eggs – 6, separated
- Light cream – 2 C.
- Coconut flour – ½ C.
- Erythritol – ½ C.
- Fresh lemon juice – 1/3 C.
- Lemon zest – 2 tsp. grated
- Lemon liquid stevia – 1 tsp.
- Salt ¼ tsp.
- Fresh blueberries ½ C.

Directions:

1) In the bowl of a stand mixer, add the egg whites and beat until stiff peaks form. Set aside.
2) In another large-sized bowl, add the egg yolks and remaining ingredients except for blueberries and beat until well blended.
3) Slowly add the whipped egg whites a little at a time and gently mix until just combined.
4) Grease the pot of a slow cooker.
5) Place the custard mixture into the prepared pot of the slow cooker and sprinkle with blueberries.
6) Close the lid of the slow cooker and set on "High" setting for 3 hours.
7) After cooking time is finished, uncover the slow cooker and transfer the custard into a large-sized bowl.
8) Set aside to cool.
9) Refrigerate for about 2 hours before serving.

Brown Rice Pudding

Cook time: 6 hours | Serves: 4 | Per Serving: Calories 238, Carbs 49.6g, Fat 3.4g, Protein 4g

Ingredients:

- Long-grain brown rice – ½ C.
- Oat milk – 1½ C.
- Unsweetened coconut milk – 1½ C.
- Maple syrup – 2 tbsp.
- Vanilla extract – 1 tsp.
- Ground cinnamon – ½ tsp.
- Salt – 1/8 tsp.
- Raisins – ½ C.

Directions:

1) In the pot of a slow cooker, add all ingredients except for raisins and stir to combine.

2) Close the lid of the slow cooker and set on "Low" setting for 4 hours.
3) After cooking time is finished, uncover the slow cooker and stir in raisins.
4) Serve warm.

Bread Pudding

Cook time: 8 hours |Serves: 4 | Per Serving: Calories 201, Carbs 27.2g, Fat 4.5g, Protein 10.9g

Ingredients:

- Fat-free milk – 2 C.
- Eggs – 3, beaten
- Applesauce – 1/3 C.
- Vanilla extract – ½ tbsp.
- Ground cinnamon – ½ tbsp.
- Whole-wheat bread slices – 4 C. cubed

Directions:

1) In a large-sized baking dish, add all ingredients except for bread cubes and beat until blended well.
2) Add bread cubes into the egg mixture and stir to combine.
3) Set aside for about 15-20 minutes.
4) Grease the pot of a slow cooker.
5) Place the bread mixture into the prepared slow cooker.
6) Close the lid of the slow cooker and set on "Low" setting for 6-8 hours.
7) After the cooking time is finished, uncover the slow cooker and serve warm.

Apple Crumble

Cook time: 4 hours |Serves: 4 | Per Serving: Calories 196, Carbs 44.7g, Fat 13.6g, Protein 5.4g

Ingredients:

- Large egg yolks – 5
- Granny Smith apples – 2, peeled, cored and cut into chunks
- Granola – ½ C.
- Bran flakes – ½ C.
- Fresh apple juice – ¼ C.
- Maple syrup – 2 tbsp.
- Unsalted butter – 2 tbsp.
- Ground cinnamon – 1 tsp.
- Ground nutmeg – ½ tsp.

Directions:

1) Grease the pot of a slow cooker.
2) In a large-sized bowl, add all ingredients and gently stir to combine.

3) Place the apple mixture into prepared slow cooker.
4) Close the lid of the slow cooker and set on "Low" setting for 4 hours.
5) After cooking time is finished, uncover the slow cooker and serve warm.

Strawberry Crumble

Cook time: 2 hours | Serves: 4 | Per Serving: Calories 291, Carbs 13.3g, Fat 24g, Protein 0.8g

Ingredients:

- Almond flour – 1 C.
- Unsalted butter – 2 tbsp. melted
- Liquid stevia – 8-10 drops
- Fresh strawberries – 3-4 C. hulled and sliced
- Unsalted butter – 1 tbsp. chopped

Directions:

1) Lightly grease the pot of a slow cooker.
2) In a large-sized bowl, add flour, melted butter and stevia and mix until a crumbly mixture forms.
3) In the pot of the prepared slow cooker, place the strawberry slices and dot with chopped butter.
4) Spread the flour mixture on top evenly.
5) Close the lid of the slow cooker and set on "Low" setting for 2 hours.
6) After cooking time is finished, uncover the slow cooker and serve warm.

Pear Cobbler

Cook time: 6 hours | Serves: 4 | Per Serving: Calories 452, Carbs 50.5g, Fat 22.2g, Protein 4.8g

Ingredients:

- Small pears – 6, cored and chopped
- Golden raisins – ½ C.
- Pine nuts – ½ C. chopped
- Ground cinnamon – 1 tbsp.
- Unsweetened almond milk – ½ C.
- Unsalted butter – 1 tbsp.
- Liquid stevia – ¼ tsp.
- Vanilla extract – 1 tsp.

Directions:

1) Grease the pot of a slow cooker.
2) In a large-sized bowl, add all ingredients and gently stir to combine.
3) Place the pear mixture into the prepared slow cooker.

4) Close the lid of the slow cooker and set on "Low" setting for 6 hours.
5) After cooking time is finished, uncover the slow cooker and serve warm.

Raspberry Cobbler

Cook time: 2 hours | Serves: 4 | Per Serving: Calories 191, Carbs 12.7g, Fat 13.6g, Protein 2.5g

Ingredients:

- Almond flour – ½ C.
- Coconut flour – 2 tbsp.
- Erythritol – 1/3 C.
- Baking soda – ½ tsp.
- Ground cinnamon – ¼ tsp.
- Pinch of salt
- Unsweetened coconut milk – 2 tbsp.
- Coconut oil – 1 tbsp.
- Small egg – 1, beaten lightly
- Fresh raspberries – 2 C.

Directions:

1) Grease the pot of a slow cooker.
2) In a large-sized bowl, blend together flours, Erythritol, baking soda, cinnamon and salt.
3) In another bowl, add the coconut milk, coconut oil and egg and beat well until blended.
4) Add the egg mixture into flour mixture and mix until just combined.
5) In the pot of the prepared slow cooker, place the flour mixture evenly and top with raspberries.
6) Close the lid of the slow cooker and set on "Low" setting for 2 hours.
7) After cooking time is finished, uncover the slow cooker and serve warm.

Mocha Cake

Cook time: 3 hours | Serves: 4 | Per Serving: Calories 423, Carbs 30.5g, Fat 29.8g, Protein 11.9g

Ingredients:

- All-purpose flour – 1 C.
- Unsweetened cocoa powder – ½ C.
- Instant coffee granules – 1 tbsp.
- Salt – ¼ tsp.
- Large eggs – 4
- Erythritol – 1½ C.
- Unsalted butter – ½ C. melted
- Vanilla extract – 1 tbsp.

Directions:

1) In a large-sized bowl, blend together flour, cocoa powder, coffee granules and salt.
2) In another large-sized bowl, add eggs, Erythritol, butter and vanilla extract and beat until well blended.
3) In the bowl of flour mixture, add the egg mixture and mix until just combined.
4) Grease the pot of a slow cooker.
5) Place the cake mixture into a greased slow cooker evenly.
6) Close the lid of the slow cooker and set on "Low" setting for 2½-3hours.
7) After the cooking time is finished, uncover the slow cooker and serve warm.

Conclusion

Slow cookers are bliss for everyone today. They make it possible for all of us to enjoy the goodness and richness of the slowly cooked meal without demanding our extra time, effort and energy. So, give your slow cookers a good try and put all the recipes from this cookbook to the test, and enjoy the best of the slow-cooked meals with friends and family.

Manufactured by Amazon.ca
Bolton, ON

30451206R00079